EDITED BY SARAH MATTHEWS

FOCUS NON-FICTION

A NEW WINDMILL COLLECTION OF NON-FICTION TEXTS

Heinemann
New Windmills

Published by Heinemann Educational Publishers
Halley Court, Jordan Hill, Oxford OX2 8EJ
A division of Reed Educational and Professional Publishing Ltd

OXFORD MELBOURNE AUCKLAND
JOHANNESBURG BLANTYRE GABORONE
IBADAN PORTSMOUTH (NH)USA CHICAGO

06 05 04 03 02
10 9 8 7 6 5 4 3 2 1

ISBN: 0 435 12890 6

Cover photographs: Atom bomb – Photodisc;
Premature baby – Science Photo Library/Mauro Fermariello;
Robotic hand – Science Photo Library/James King-Holmes;
Scorpion – Corbis/Mark L Stephenson.
Cover design by The Point
Photographs: p82 Andes Press Agency/Carlos Reyes Manzo; p91 Trustees of
Burston Strike School; p.98 Robert Harding Picture Library/Mark Mawson;
p.121 Impact Photos/Simon Shepheard; p.136 Impact Photos/Mark Cator;
p.161 PA Photos; p.193 Impact Photos/Simon Shepheard; p.200 Topham
Picturepoint/The Image Works/Tom Brakefield.
Typeset by Tek-Art, Croydon, Surrey
Printed and bound in the United Kingdom by Clays Ltd, St Ives plc

Tel: 01865 888058 www.heinemann.co.uk

Contents

Introduction for students

There is an awful lot of writing in the world and it may sometimes feel like you are expected to read it all this week! How can you make sense of it, so that you can read it with understanding and so that your own writing is clear and appropriate? One way is to divide it into bite-sized chunks. But how do you divide up texts? A simple way is to separate them into fiction and non-fiction – fiction being made-up stories and non-fiction being everything else.

This book aims to help you find your way around non-fiction texts by grouping them together in four main areas according to what the writers are trying to do – what their *purpose* is. Texts by writers who are trying simply to entertain their readers or who are interested in exploring their own experiences appear in Section 1. Texts by writers who are seeking to give their readers information, or to explain or describe something appear in Section 2. Section 3 contains texts by writers who are arguing a case, advising their readers or seeking to persuade them of a point of view. Section 4 contains texts written to analyse a situation or event, or to comment on them.

The extracts and activities will help you gradually build up a picture of the way in which different purposes lead to different kinds of writing, with different uses of vocabulary and sentence structure.

The range of extracts in this book covers various aspects of human activities and experiences from various points of view. I hope you will find some that connect with your own interests, and many that inform, excite and even, on occasion, amuse you.

Sarah Matthews

Introduction for teachers

The texts in this book have been selected to meet three criteria:

- as examples of the different genres of writing set out in the National Curriculum requirements
- to link with the reading, writing, and speaking and listening strands of the Literacy Framework, and
- to carry a theme across four different genres of writing to enable the analysis of differences between genres.

Of course, it is not always straightforward to decide the generic category to which a particular text belongs; a text may describe and entertain, analyse and argue. The categorisation in this selection has been carried out on a 'best fit' basis, following the main focus of the purpose of each text. There is no strictly imaginative writing in this collection, since that is more the domain of fiction, poetry and drama, but there is a selection of texts here written both to explore and entertain. The categorisation and focus of each text is given on page vii.

This book contains a number of activities. Some of these appear at the end of each section and explore the genre of writing in that section. These activities can be carried out before, during and after reading any or all of the texts in that genre. The remaining activities appear in Section 5 at the end of the book (see pages 228–245). Here, students are invited to make comparisons between the genres set out according to theme, and to replicate one or more of those genres in their writing. Each of the activities is linked to the Literacy Framework as shown on page viii.

The texts selected range in difficulty from the very straightforward to the highly sophisticated. They have been set out within each section in order of difficulty, so that students may encounter the most straightforward passages first.

A few of the texts deal with sensitive subjects, such as the death of a loved one or different approaches to sexual relationships, which are very relevant to students, but which may also be felt to require a level of emotional maturity on the part of the student or increased intervention by the teacher in order to be fully understood.

The selection includes writing from different cultures and other times, including some pre-1914 writing.

This collection does not pretend to be exhaustive, but it does seek to provide some interesting and unusual insights into a range of experiences, attitudes and events all of which are relevant to young people today.

Sarah Matthews

Categorisation and focus of texts

	imagine, explore, entertain	inform, explain, describe	persuade, argue, advise	analyse, review, comment
Travel	1.12 London: the City-Stage *entertain*	2.10 Soaking in Port Sunlight *describe*	3.6 Respecting Islam *advise*	4.11 My Own Private Tokyo *analyse*
Social issues	1.7 Learning to be Poor *explore*	2.12 Every Breath You Take *inform*	3.8 Resistance is the Secret of Joy *argue*	4.5 Social Crisis 1991 *analyse*
Nature	1.2 A Charm of Scorpions *explore/entertain*	2.2 First Aid For Your Cat *inform*	3.4 Going Fox Hunting *advise*	4.7 Where Have All the Tigers Gone? *comment*
Extreme experiences	1.8 Are We Related? *explore*	2.9 With Austrian Cavalry on the Eastern Front *describe*	3.3 Winter in Canada – We Love It! *persuade*	4.8 Becoming a Patient *analyse*
School	1.3 Potatoes and Presents *explore/entertain*	2.5 When the Kids Were United *explain*	3.1 Incredibly Naughty Ways to Survive Work and Lessons at School *advise*	4.9 Dossing, Blagging and Wagging *analyse*
Childhood	1.4 Useless Presents and a Few Small Aunts *entertain*	2.3 'I'm Too Poor To Go To School' *explain*	3.7 Surviving Adolescence *advise*	4.10 Children of the Middle Class *comment*
Romance	1.5 Love and Liver Sausage *explore*	2.8 The Philosophy of Catching Your Man *explain*	3.9 Romance: An Address to Girls *persuade*	4.6 Romance and Sex on Holidays Abroad *analyse*
Birth and death	1.10 One in a Hundred *explore*	2.6 The Truth About New Babies *inform*	3.5 Coping With Death *advise*	4.4 Rabbiting *comment*
Hobbies and pastimes	1.1 Lollies *entertain*	2.7 Orienteering *describe*	3.11 How To Be An Artistic Genius *advise*	4.1 Tending Roses and Feeding Foxes *review*
Occupations	1.6 Overgrown Boys *explore/entertain*	2.1 David Beckham *describe*	3.2 Career Guidance *advise*	4.3 Red Hot England Fire Famous Five *review*
Science	1.9 The Animal-Watcher *explore*	2.4 Where in the World Are We? *inform*	3.12 Like Human, Like Machine *argue*	4.2 Saving the World *review*
War	1.11 City of Corpses *explore*	2.11 Visiting Hiroshima *describe*	3.10 Some Necessary Changes in Outlook *argue*	4.12 The Decision to Use the Bomb *analyse*

Links between activities and the Literacy Framework

Focus	Questions	Year 7	Year 8	Year 9
Section 1				
Writing to entertain	1, 2, 3	V14, R7, R14, W7, W14, S&L1, S&L13	S9, V11, R10, W6, S&L10	R6, W6, W7, S&L10
Writing to explore	1, 2, 3	S13b, V20, R6, R8, W6, W7, S&L1, S&L13	S7, R5, W6, S&L10	V8, R11, W5, W6, W7, S&L10
Writing to explore and entertain	1, 2, 3	S13b, R6, R14, W7, S&L1, S&L13	R4, W6, S&L10	R1, W6, W7, S&L10
Section 2				
Writing to inform	1, 2, 3	S8, S13a, V20, R7, W10, W13, S&L1, S&L13	S6, V10, R10, W10, S&L10	S1, V8, R1, R11, W9, W11, S&L10
Writing to explain	1, 2, 3	S8, S9, S13c, V20, R7, W12, S&L1, S&L13	S6, S7, V10, R3, R10, W11, S&L10	R3, W10, S&L10
Writing to describe	1, 2, 3	S10, R2, R7, W14, S&L1, S&L13	S7, V11, R5, W12, S&L10	V7, R3, W11, S&L10
Section 3				
Writing to persuade	1, 2, 3	S10, S13e, R1, R4, R7, W15, S&L1, S&L13	S7, V11, R3, R6, W13, S&L10	S7, V7, R3, R4, R11, R12, W13, S&L10
Writing to argue	1, 2, 3	S9, S13e, R1, R4, R7, R9, W16, S&L1, S&L13	S6, S7, V13, R1, R2, R3, R6, W14, S&L10	V7, R2, R3, R4, R7, W14, S&L10
Writing to advise	1, 2, 3	S9, S10, S20, R1, R2, R4, R6, R13, W17, S&L1, S&L13	S2, S6, S7, S9, V10, R1, R2, R3, W15, S&L10	V7, V8, R1, R2, R3, R4, W15, S&L10

Focus	Questions	Year 7	Year 8	Year 9
Section 4				
Writing to analyse	1, 2, 3	S8, S9, S10, S14, V21, R1, R2, R3, R4, R9, W18, S&L1, S&L13	S6, S7, S8, V7c, V9, R1, R6, W16, W17 S&L3, S&L5, S&L10	S3, R2, W16, S&L5, S&L7, S&L10
Writing to review	1, 2, 3	S8, S9, S10, S11, S13f, S14, V21, R1, R2, R3, R4, R7, R10, R11, R13, W19,	S6, S7, S8, V12, R3, W16, W17, W18, S&L10	S6, S7, R3, R11, R18, W16, W17, S&L10, S&L1, S&L13
Writing to comment	1, 2, 3	S8, S9, S10, S11, S13f, S14, R1, R2, R3, R4, R10, W18, W19, S&L1, S&L13	S6, S7, S9, S10, S12, R1, R2, R3, R6, R8, W16, W17, W18 S&L10	S6, R1, R2, R3, R4, R7, R11, W16, W17, S&L10
Section 5				
Writing to entertain, describe, advise, analyse	1	S14, V14, R3, S&L1, S&L13*	S8, S9, V7c, V12, R1, R3, R8, S&L10*	S6, V7, R2, R3, R7, R10, S&L10*
Writing to explore, inform, argue, analyse	2	S14, V14, R3, S&L1, S&L13*	S8, S9, V7c, V12, R1, R3, R8, S&L10*	S6, V7, R2, R3, R7, R10, S&L10*
Writing to explore and entertain, inform, advise, comment	3	S14, V14, R3, S&L1, S&L13*	S8, S9, V7c, V12, R1, R3, R8, S&L10*	S6, V7, R2, R3, R7, R10, S&L10*
Writing to explore, describe, persuade, analyse	4	S14, V14, R3, S&L1, S&L13*	S8, S9, V7c, V12, R1, R3, R8, S&L10*	S6, V7, R2, R3, R7, R10, S&L10*

Focus	Questions	Year 7	Year 8	Year 9
Writing to explore and entertain, explain, advise, analyse	5	S14, V14, R3, S&L1, S&L13*	S8, S9, V7c, V12, R1, R3, R8, S&L10*	S6, V7, R2, R3, R7, R10, S&L10*
Writing to entertain, explain, advise, comment	6	S14, V14, R3, S&L1, S&L13*	S8, S9, V7c, V12, R1, R3, R8, S&L10*	S6, V7, R2, R3, R7, R10, S&L10*
Writing to explore, explain, persuade, analyse	7	S14, V14, R3, S&L1, S&L13*	S8, S9, V7c, V12, R1, R3, R8, S&L10*	S6, V7, R2, R3, R7, R10, S&L10*
Writing to explore, inform, advise, comment	8	S14, V14, R3, S&L1, S&L13*	S8, S9, V7c, V12, R1, R3, R8, S&L10*	S6, V7, R2, R3, R7, R10, S&L10*
Writing to entertain, describe, advise, review	9	S14, V14, R3, S&L1, S&L13*	S8, S9, V7c, V12, R1, R3, R8, S&L10*	S6, V7, R2, R3, R7, R10, S&L10*
Writing to explore and entertain, describe, advise, review	10	S14, V14, R3, S&L1, S&L13*	S8, S9, V7c, V12, R1, R3, R8, S&L10*	S6, V7, R2, R3, R7, R10, S&L10*
Writing to explore, inform, argue, review	11	S14, V14, R3, S&L1, S&L13*	S8, S9, V7c, V12, R1, R3, R8, S&L10*	S6, V7, R2, R3, R7, R10, S&L10*
Writing to explore, describe, argue, analyse	12	S14, V14, R3, S&L1, S&L13*	S8, S9, V7c, V12, R1, R3, R8, S&L10*	S6, V7, R2, R3, R7, R10, S&L10*

* The Framework Objectives for each of the genres are also met in these activities.

Section 1
Writing to imagine, explore, entertain

Although some of the texts in this section are written by imaginative writers (novelists and poets), none of them is really an imaginative text. That belongs more to fiction-writing. Here the writers are concerned with exploring aspects of their personal experience with a greater or lesser emphasis on entertaining the reader.

To some extent, writing to explore can be seen as writing that the writer is doing for him or herself in order to record or understand something. The reader is less directly addressed than in other forms of non-fiction writing. It is more as if the reader is looking over the writer's shoulder and peeking into his or her private world.

In writing to entertain, on the other hand, the writer is trying to present the topic so that the reader will enjoy reading about it. The reader here is more like an audience at a magic show, with the writer doing tricks to amaze them or telling jokes to make them laugh.

The third kind of text in this section, writing that both explores and entertains, draws on past experience that the writer finds odd or amusing. It is still a private experience, but shown to the reader with a deliberately humorous slant.

Extract 1.1
Clive James was born and brought up in Australia. In this passage he remembers going to the cinema as a boy, and the sweets that he would eat there.

Lollies

When you got to the Odeon the first thing you did was stock up with lollies. Lollies was the word for what the English call sweets and the Americans call candy. Some of the more privileged children had upwards of five shillings each to dispose of, but in fact two **bob** was enough to buy you as much as you could eat. Everyone, without exception, bought at least one Hoadley's Violet Crumble Bar. It was a slab of dense, dry honeycomb coated with chocolate. So **frangible** was the honeycomb that it would shatter when bitten, scattering bright yellow **shrapnel**. It was like trying to eat a **Ming vase**. The honeycomb would go soft only after a day's exposure to direct sunlight. The chocolate surrounding it, however, would liquefy after only ten minutes in a dark cinema.

Fantails came in a weird, blue, rhomboidal packet shaped like an isosceles triangle with one corner missing. Each individual Fantail was wrapped in a piece of paper detailing a film star's biography – hence the pun, fan tales. The Fantail itself was a chocolate-coated toffee so glutinous that it could induce lockjaw in a mule. People had to have their mouths chipped open with a cold

---

bob: slang for shilling, worth roughly 60p today
frangible: breakable
shrapnel: bomb fragments
Ming vase: very fragile vase from the time of the Ming dynasty in China

chisel. One packet of Fantails would last an average human being for ever. A group of six small boys could get through a packet during the course of a single afternoon at the pictures, but it took hard work and a lot of strangled crying in the dark. Any fillings you had in your second teeth would be removed instantly, while children who still had any first teeth left didn't keep them long.

The star lolly, outstripping even the Violet Crumble Bar and the Fantail in popularity, was undoubtedly the Jaffa. A packet of Jaffas was loaded like a cluster bomb with about fifty globular lollies the size of ordinary marbles. The Jaffa had a dark chocolate core and a brittle orange candy coat: in cross section it looked rather like the planet Earth. It presented two alternative ways of being eaten, each with its allure. You could fondle the Jaffa on the tongue until your saliva ate its way through the casing, whereupon the taste of chocolate would invade your mouth with a sublime, majestic inevitability. Or you could bite straight through and submit the interior of your head to a stunning explosion of flavour. Sucking and biting your way through forty or so Jaffas while Jungle Jim wrestled with crocodiles, you nearly always had a few left over after the stomach could take no more. The spare Jaffas made ideal ammunition. Flying through the dark, they would bounce off an infantile skull with the noise of bullets hitting a bell. They showered on the stage when the manager came out to **announce the lucky ticket**. The Jaffa is a part of Australia's theatrical heritage. There was a famous occasion, during the Borovansky Ballet production of *Giselle* at the Tivoli in Sydney, when **Albrecht** was forced to abandon the performance. It was a

---

announce the lucky ticket: cinema tickets were numbered, and one number, picked at random, won a prize at the end of the show
Albrecht: a character in the ballet, a duke in love with the peasant girl Giselle

special afternoon presentation of the ballet before an audience of schoolchildren. Lying in a swoon while awaiting the reappearance of Giselle, Albrecht aroused much comment because of his **protuberant codpiece**. After being hit square on the power-bulge by a speeding Jaffa, he woke up with a rush and hopped off the stage in the stork position.

Clive James, *Unreliable Memoirs*

---

protuberant: bulging, prominent
codpiece: protection worn by male ballet dancers under their tights, rather like the cricket-boxes and jockstraps worn by cricketers and other male athletes

Extract 1.2
Gerald Durrell was a well-known naturalist and writer about the natural world. He was one of the first people to set up a zoo to care for endangered species. In a book called *My Family and Other Animals* he describes his childhood on the Greek island of Corfu, where he lived with his mother, sister and two brothers.

A Charm of Scorpions

The crumbling wall that surrounded the sunken garden alongside the house was a rich hunting ground for me. It was an ancient brick wall that had been plastered over, but now this outer skin was green with moss, bulging and sagging with the damp of many winters.

The inhabitants of the wall were a mixed lot, and they were divided into day and night workers, the hunters and the hunted. The shyest and most self-effacing of the wall community were the most dangerous; you hardly ever saw one unless you looked for it, and yet there must have been several hundred living in the cracks of the wall. Slide a knife-blade carefully under a piece of loose plaster and lever it gently away from the brick, and there, crouching beneath it, would be a little black scorpion an inch long, looking as though he were made out of polished chocolate. They were weird-looking things, with their flattened, oval bodies, their neat, crooked legs, the enormous, crab-like claws, **bulbous** and neatly jointed as armour, and the tail like a string of brown beads ending in a sting like a rose-thorn. The scorpion would lie there quite quietly as you examined him, only raising his tail in

bulbous: bulb-shaped, bulging

an almost apologetic gesture of warning if you breathed too hard on him.

I grew very fond of these scorpions. I found them to be pleasant, unassuming creatures with, on the whole, the most charming habits. Provided you did nothing silly or clumsy (like putting your hand on one) the scorpions treated you with respect, their one desire being to get away and hide as quickly as possible. They must have found me rather a trial, for I was always ripping sections of the plaster away so that I could watch them, or capturing them and making them walk about in jam-jars so that I could see the way their feet moved. By means of my sudden and unexpected assaults on the wall I discovered quite a bit about scorpions. I found they would eat bluebottles (though how they caught them was a mystery I never solved), grasshoppers, moths, and lacewing-flies. Several times I found them eating each other, a habit I found most distressing in a creature otherwise so **impeccable**.

By crouching under the wall at night with a torch, I managed to catch some brief glimpses of the scorpions' wonderful courtship dances. I saw them standing, claws clasped, their bodies raised to the skies, their tails lovingly entwined; I saw them waltzing in slow circles among the moss cushions, claw in claw. But my view of these performances was all too short, for almost as soon as I switched on the torch the partners would stop, pause for a moment, and then, seeing that I was not going to extinguish the light, they would turn round and walk firmly away, claw in claw, side by side. They were definitely beasts that believed in keeping themselves *to* themselves. If I could have kept a colony in captivity I would probably have been able to see the whole of the courtship, but the family had forbidden scorpions in the house, despite my arguments in favour of them.

---

impeccable: unable to do wrong

Then one day I found a fat female scorpion in the wall, wearing what at first glance appeared to be a pale fawn fur coat. Closer inspection proved that this strange garment was made up of a mass of tiny babies clinging to the mother's back. I was enraptured by this family, and I made up my mind to smuggle them into the house and up to my bedroom so that I might keep them and watch them grow up. With infinite care I manoeuvred the mother and family into a matchbox, and then hurried to the villa. It was rather unfortunate that just as I entered the door lunch should be served; however, I placed the matchbox carefully on the mantelpiece in the drawing-room, so that the scorpions should get plenty of air, and made my way to the dining-room and joined the family for the meal. Dawdling over my food, feeding **Roger** surreptitiously under the table and listening to the family arguing, I completely forgot about my exciting new captures. At last **Larry**, having finished, fetched the cigarettes from the drawing-room, and lying back in his chair he put one in his mouth and picked up the matchbox he had brought. Oblivious of my impending doom I watched him interestedly as, still talking **glibly**, he opened the matchbox.

Now I maintain to this day that the female scorpion meant no harm. She was agitated and a trifle annoyed at being shut up in a matchbox for so long, and so she seized the first opportunity to escape. She hoisted herself out of the box with great rapidity, her babies clinging on desperately, and scuttled on to the back of Larry's hand. There, not quite certain what to do next, she paused, her sting curved up at the ready. Larry, feeling the movement of her claws, glanced down to see what it was, and from that moment things got increasingly confused.

Roger: the family dog
Larry: the writer's elder brother
glibly: smoothly

He uttered a roar of fright that made **Lugaretzia** drop a plate and brought Roger out from beneath the table, barking wildly. With a flick of his hand he sent the unfortunate scorpion flying down the table, and she landed midway between **Margo** and **Leslie**, scattering babies like confetti as she thumped on the cloth. Thoroughly enraged at this treatment, the creature sped towards Leslie, her sting quivering with emotion. Leslie leapt to his feet, overturning his chair, and flicked out desperately with his napkin, sending the scorpion rolling across the table towards Margo, who promptly let out a scream that any railway engine would have been proud to produce. Mother, completely bewildered by this sudden and rapid change from peace to chaos, put on her glasses and peered down at the table to see what was causing the pandemonium, and at that moment Margo, in a vain attempt to stop the scorpion's advance, hurled a glass of water at it. The shower missed the animal completely, but successfully drenched Mother, who, not being able to stand cold water, promptly lost her breath and sat gasping at the end of the table, unable even to protest. The scorpion had now gone to ground under Leslie's plate, while her babies swarmed wildly all over the table. Roger, mystified by the panic, but determined to do his share, ran round and round the room, barking hysterically.

'It's that bloody boy again . . .' bellowed Larry.

'Look out! Look out! They're coming!' screamed Margo.

'All we need is a book,' roared Leslie; 'don't panic, hit 'em with a book.'

'What on earth's the *matter* with you all?' Mother kept imploring, mopping her glasses.

Since no one had bothered to explain things to him, Roger was under the mistaken impression that the family

---

Lugaretzia: the family's Greek cook and housekeeper
Margo: the writer's older sister
Leslie: the writer's other brother

were being attacked, and that it was his duty to defend them. As Lugaretzia was the only stranger in the room, he came to the logical conclusion that she must be the responsible party, so he bit her on the ankle. This did not help matters.

By the time a certain amount of order had been restored, all the baby scorpions had hidden themselves under various plates and bits of cutlery. Eventually, after impassioned pleas on my part, backed up by Mother, Leslie's suggestion that the whole lot be slaughtered was **quashed**. While the family, still simmering with rage and fright, retired to the drawing-room, I spent half an hour rounding up the babies, picking them up in a teaspoon, and returning them to their mother's back. Then I carried them outside on a saucer and, with the utmost reluctance, released them on the garden wall. Roger and I went and spent the afternoon on the hillside, for I felt it would be **prudent** to allow the family to have a **siesta** before seeing them again.

The results of this incident were numerous. Larry developed a phobia about matchboxes and opened them with the utmost caution, a handkerchief wrapped round his hand. Lugaretzia limped round the house, her ankle enveloped in yards of bandages, for weeks after the bite had healed, and came round every morning, with the tea, to show us how the scabs were getting on. But, from my point of view, the worst **repercussion** of the whole affair was that Mother decided I was running wild again, and that it was high time I received a little more education.

Gerald Durrell, from *The Best of Gerald Durrell* chosen by Lee Durrell

---

quashed: thrown out, rejected
prudent: sensible
siesta: afternoon sleep
repercussion: result

Extract 1.3
Laurie Lee was a poet and writer. Perhaps his most famous book is ***Cider with Rosie***, an account of his childhood in Gloucestershire. In the passage below, he describes his first day at school at the age of four.

Potatoes and Presents

The village school at that time provided all the instruction we were likely to ask for. It was a small stone barn divided by a wooden partition into two rooms – The Infants and The Big Ones . . . The morning came, without any warning, when my sisters surrounded me, wrapped me in scarves, tied up my bootlaces, thrust a cap on my head, and stuffed a baked potato in my pocket.

'What's this?' I said.

'You're starting school today.'

I arrived at the school just three feet tall and fatly wrapped in my scarves. The playground roared like a rodeo. Tall girls with frizzled hair, and huge boys with sharp elbows, began to prod me with hideous interest. They plucked at my scarves, spun me round like a top, screwed my nose, and stole my potato.

I was rescued at last by a gracious lady – the sixteen year-old junior-teacher – who boxed a few ears and dried my face and led me off to The Infants. I spent that first day picking holes in paper, then went home in a smouldering temper.

'What's the matter, Loll? Didn't he like it at school, then?'

'They never gave me the present!'

'Present? What present?'

'They said they'd give me a present!'

'Well, now, I'm sure they didn't.'

'They did! They said: "You're Laurie Lee, ain't you? Well, just sit there for the present." I sat there all day but I never got it. I ain't going back there again!'

Laurie Lee, *Cider with Rosie*

Extract 1.4

Dylan Thomas was a famous Welsh poet who loved using words in exciting and unusual ways. Here he is describing his memories of Christmas as a small boy. As you read through, have a look at how many comparisons Thomas uses, and how they help to build up a picture in the reader's mind.

Useless Presents and a Few Small Aunts

A small boy says: 'It snowed last year, too. I made a snowman and my brother knocked it down and I knocked my brother down and then we had tea.'

'But that was not the same snow,' I say. 'Our snow was not only shaken from whitewash buckets down the sky, it came shawling out of the ground and swam and drifted out of the arms and hands and bodies of the trees; snow grew overnight on the roofs of houses like a pure and grandfather moss, minutely white-ivied the walls and settled on the postman, opening the gate, like a dumb, numb thunderstorm of white, torn Christmas cards.'

'Were there postmen then, too?'

'With sprinkling eyes and wind-cherried noses, on spread, frozen feet they crunched up to the doors and mittened on them manfully.

'And then they stood on the white Welcome mat in the little, drifted porches and huffed and puffed, making ghosts with their breath, and jogged from foot to foot like small boys wanting to go out.'

'And then the Presents?'

'And then the Presents, after the Christmas box. And the cold postman, with a rose on his button-nose, tingled down the tea-tray-slithered run of the chilly glinting hill. He went in his ice-bound boots like a man on fishmonger's slabs. He wagged his bag like a frozen camel's hump, dizzily turned the corner on one foot, and, by God, he was gone.'

'Get back to the Presents.'

'There were the Useful Presents: engulfing mufflers of the old coach days, and mittens made for giant sloths; zebra scarfs of a substance like silky gum that could be tug-o'-warred down to the **galoshes**; blinding **tam-o'-shanters** like patchwork tea cosies and bunny-suited **busbies** and **balaclavas** for victims of head-shrinking tribes; from aunts who always wore wool next to the skin there were moustached and rasping vests that made you wonder why the aunts had any skin left at all; and once I had a little crocheted nose bag from an aunt now, alas, no longer whinnying with us. And pictureless books in which small boys, though warned with quotations not to, *would* skate on Farmer Giles' pond and did and drowned; and books that told me everything about the wasp, except why.'

'Go on to the Useless Presents.'

'Bags of moist and many-coloured jelly babies and a folded flag and a false nose and a tram-conductor's cap and a machine that punched tickets and rang a bell; never a catapult; once, by a mistake that no one could explain, a little hatchet; and a celluloid duck that made, when you pressed it, a most unducklike sound, a mewing moo that an ambitious cat might make who wished to be a cow; and a painting book in which I could make the grass, the trees, the sea and the animals any colour I pleased, and still the dazzling sky-blue sheep are grazing in the red field under the rainbow-billed and pea-green birds.

'Hardboileds, toffee, fudge and allsorts, crunches, cracknels, humbugs, glaciers, marzipan, and butterwelsh

---

galoshes: rubber overshoes
tam-o'-shanters, busbies and balaclavas: different kinds of hats

for the Welsh. And troops of bright tin soldiers who, if they could not fight, could always run. And Snakes-and-Families and Happy Ladders. And Easy Hobbi-Games for Little Engineers, complete with instructions.

'Oh, easy for **Leonardo**! And a whistle to make the dogs bark to wake up the old man next door to make him beat on the wall with his stick to shake our picture off the wall.

'And a packet of **cigarettes**; you put one in your mouth and you stood at the corner of the street and you waited for hours, in vain, for an old lady to scold you for smoking a cigarette, and then with a smirk you ate it. And then it was breakfast under the balloons.'

'Were there Uncles like in our house?'

'There are always Uncles at Christmas.

'The same Uncles. And on Christmas mornings, with dog-disturbing whistle and sugar fags, I would scour the swatched town for the news of the little world, and find always a dead bird by the white Post Office or by the deserted swings; perhaps a robin, all but one of his fires out. Men and women wading or scooping back from chapel, with **taproom** noses and wind-**bussed** cheeks, all **albinos**, huddled their stiff black jarring feathers against the irreligious snow.

'Mistletoe hung from the gas brackets in all the front parlours; there was sherry and walnuts and bottled beer

---

Leonardo: Leonardo da Vinci (1452–1519), a great Italian artist and inventor

cigarettes: a children's sweet of white sugar-sticks with red ends, packaged to look like cigarettes

taproom: a room in a pub; the people's noses, red from the cold, made them look as if they had been drinking

bussed: kissed

albinos: people without pigmentation (colour) in their skin, eyes and hair

and crackers by the dessertspoons; and cats in their fur-abouts watched the fires; and the high-heaped fire spat, all ready for the chestnuts and the mulling pokers.

'Some few large men sat in the front parlours, without their collars, Uncles almost certainly, trying their new cigars, holding them out judiciously at arms' length, returning them to their mouths, coughing, then holding them out again as though waiting for the explosion; and some few small Aunts, not wanted in the kitchen, nor anywhere else for that matter, sat on the very edges of their chairs, poised and brittle, afraid to break, like faded cups and saucers.'

Dylan Thomas, *A Child's Christmas in Wales*

Extract 1.5

At the beginning of the Second World War, Joan Wyndham was a young woman living in London, training at art school. She divided her time between her painting, working at a first-aid post and seeing the young men in her life. This is an extract from her diary.

Love and Liver Sausage

July 24th, 1940

Rupert to lunch at my place. Liver sausage, salad and tea. It was terribly hot so we went to the Serpentine to swim.

Blue water, green grass, brown shoulders. I think this is heaven. I turned over to tan my front and saw Rupert, who had just come out of the changing hut, looking like a Greek god, bronzed all over in the scantiest of trunks; and not a hair on his chest! I would have fallen over backwards, if I hadn't been on my back already. He was certainly the best-looking man there, his dark beard and hair giving him the air of a young Hebrew king. He has an **aquiline** nose that curves down slightly at the tip, but I don't think he is Jewish. I like the way his neck sockets into his chest, and the curving line of his collarbone. Oh boy, oh boy! ...

'By the way,' asked Rupert, as we sat in the cafeteria and ate a Lyon's fresh cream sandwich for tea, 'why are you a virgin?'

'I don't really know,' I said. 'It's never occurred to

---

aquiline: sharp and pointed, shaped like an eagle's beak me to be anything else.'

He picked up my hand and studied my palm. 'I think it's because you sit aloof in an ivory tower, like me … It does make life very boring, this aloof attitude. I expect if you had been more of the milling and beetling kind Gerhardt would have seduced you, in spite of everything. You're like me, you look as if you're always expecting something to happen, but it doesn't unless you make it. I'm the same, I bore myself to tears, but I'm far too lazy to try and make contact with life.'

When I got up to go home at six he said, 'How would you like it if I robbed you of your virginity?'

I thought for a minute.

'I don't *think* I should mind very much, but then I hardly know you well enough to say.'

September 25th, 1940

By this morning I had worked myself into such a state of passion over the absent Rupert – I hadn't seen him for a week – that I didn't know what to do with myself. All morning at the post I was thinking about him and wondering how much longer I could bear life without him.

On the way home I saw seventeen German planes in arrow formation cutting through the blue sky, with hundreds of shells bursting around them. The guns were so loud I took shelter in the door of the **Servite church**. As I was cowering there I heard a yell – 'Woo hoo! Joanie!' – and there was old R. lurching down the

---

Servite church: a Catholic church for nuns or monks of the Order of the Servants of the Blessed Mary

street with a cheery smile on his face, completely ignoring the guns.

'Lunch?' he said happily, pushing me ahead of him just as if nothing was happening. He was all brown and glowing, his thin cheeks flushed like pomegranates, talking about *Heloïse and Abelard*, which he had been reading at his ma's – that is, he read all the sexy bits and skipped the rest. We brewed coffee on the oil stove, while I sat on the edge of his chair with my arms round his neck. He looked around the studio appreciatively. 'Gosh, you have cleaned the place up – you know this studio's quite classy now. It used to be a howling wilderness where Jo and his cronies painted – now he'd damn well have to take his boots off before coming! Would you say your artistic career has come to a grinding halt? I don't seem to see the usual dreadful paintings around.'

I explained that what with the bombs and working at the first-aid post I really didn't have time for art any more.

'All the more time for looking after Rooples,' he chortled with satisfaction. I choked down my happiness and got lunch ready. Rupert had bought **minute steak** – it took the whole of his **meat ration**. I hadn't had any for weeks. He set about frying the onions and I sat watching him, marvelling more and

---

minute steak: a very thin cut of beef-steak, so-called because it is supposed to take only a minute to cook

meat ration: during the Second World War, all food in Britain was rationed, with a set amount that each person could buy in a week

more at his extraordinary physical charm. Why the handsomest man in Chelsea and Fulham should want to sit around my dump frying onions is more than I can fathom …

Boy, what a steak! And what onions!

After we had eaten he wanted to lie down with me but I resisted, and we crashed down together on to the sofa, most undignified.

'Now this here Heloïse,' Rupert said reprovingly, sitting on my stomach. 'She used to *glide* down to Abelard's couch – in fact she spent most of her time doing it, clad only in a loose-bodied gown and carrying a lamp. Now let's see you glide down to me, Joanie, ten stone or no ten stone.' Looking v. intense, I glided. 'You know I think I almost missed you,' R. said.

After that we quit being funny and made love very seriously, and I was filled with peace and delight. You can't write about sensuality mingled with tenderness and pity, it just becomes maudlin or goes bad on you in some way – so call it love and leave it at that, one of the few **transcendent** and satisfying things left in this bloody awful life.

Joan Wyndham, *Love Lessons: A Wartime Diary*

---

transcendent: extraordinary, more beautiful than the usual

Extract 1.6

Writing in the football magazine *FourFourTwo*, Steven Wells explores the reasons why so many enthusiastic young football players stop playing when they grow up.

Overgrown Boys. Armanis for Goalposts. Isn't it?

Grown-up kickabouts? That would be nice,
says Steven Wells

Peel Park, Bradford, 1973, three-star tank tops for goalposts …

The sweat-drenched legs of your Wrangler flares flap savagely as you weave past the giant elephant turds left by the recently departed Billy Smart's Circus and tee up a Bobby Charlton scorcher but CRUNCH! Look out! It's Norman Hunter wannabe Gaz, out of his tree on **Woodpecker** and smoking one of the Park Drives he snaffled off his mam. He gets your legs, he gets the ball and – WHOOMPH! – he gets third degree burns as the economy box of **Swan Vestas** secreted in the right thigh pocket of his natty green **waisters** ignites. He screams in agony as you join the rest of your mates in kicking out the flames.

'Right lads! Any chance of a game?' It's a drunk, an adult. You ignore him. Grown-ups always spoil football. They might mean well but they always start shouting nonsense like 'mark your man!', 'stay in position!', 'use the channels!' or some other gibberish. The drunk's pleading turns to abuse but we continue

---

Woodpecker: a kind of cider
Swan Vestas: a brand of matches

to ignore him and eventually he staggers off, leaving us to our George Best dribbles, our Lorimer hot-shots and our Chopper Harris-style two-footed lunges. For we are in heaven, little knowing that we will never again be this happy – until the dinnertime 40-a-side no-rules epic played with a disintegrating tennis ball on the tarmac basketball court on the first day back at school. But, apart from that, it's pretty much downhill from that day on.

Football is meant to be our national sport but, as the fishing community are so fond of reminding us, more men go angling on a weekend than actually play the game. In fact most adult males – including most of the keenest spectators – would rather gnaw their own legs off than trot out on a pitch themselves. And with good reason. So who's ruined football? Eh? I'll tell you. It's not Zoë Ball. Or Man Utd. No, it's men.

First come the PE teachers with their insane obsession with systems and tactics. Brian Glover's cameo in *Kes* wasn't a parody, it was artfully understated docu-drama. They make you stick to a position, they insist on playing in the winter, in the snow and in the rain (for God's sake why?). The barking idiots dreamed of discovering and nurturing another Stanley Matthews but instead they created yet another generation of soft lads whose abiding memory of the beautiful game is the agonising sting of a sleet-sodden leather caser slapping into red-raw thighs. Next come the lads who were good at football. In later years we make heroes of these oafs but we forget what these idiots were like at school. Swaggering bullies every one. They got the girls, they got

Kes: a film in which Brian Glover played a PE teacher

trials at Bradford City or Halifax and then most of them got jobs as coppers or middle managers.

But despite this coalition of thugs and power junkies, I carried on playing. Fags and beer cut into my stamina, and sex and punk rock reared their ugly heads – but nothing compared to the buzz to be got from belting around a pitch for 90 minutes without making a complete idiot of yourself. But it's now that I start to meet, in seemingly ever-increasing numbers, the real reason most men stop playing football. I am talking, of course, of the Park Football Psychopath.

Fast forward. It's 1991. I've been drafted into a scratch team of left-wing newspaper sellers, musicians and social workers. Our opposition are farmers. We're rubbish. None of us are taking it seriously. To be honest, none of us are capable of taking it that seriously. Roger, our saxophone-playing, 6ft 3 central defender, is puking up last night's Guinness after five minutes, and we're already 3–0 down. It's the first game of football I've played for 20 years and I'm soon remembering why I stopped.

The opposition are screaming at us. They're screaming at each other. They're screaming at the proverbial bloke with a dog who constitutes the crowd. And they're screaming at the bloke's dog, the referee and the linesmen. Halfway through the first half we're 8–0 down. Then Martin, our most skilful and fittest player, gets his first touch. He sprints towards the opposition goal. Past one lunging tackle, past another and then, inevitably, he's hacked off his feet. He gets the ball from the free kick and – wallop – he's elbowed in the face. Twenty seconds later he's floored by a punch to the back of the head. And that's when you remember why you stopped playing the game you love.

Five years later I started playing six-a-side on Sundays. Anyone could turn up and get a game – as long as they were pathetic, unfit and willing to play their well-padded guts out. And pay £3, obviously. We got quite good. We started challenging other teams of fat lads and, eventually, we even started beating them. And then some bright spark enrolled us in a proper organised tournament, and we re-entered a world of pain. We should have been warned by the fact that the opposition in our first game were dressed in immaculate Arsenal strips (rather than the motley collection of rock band promo T-shirts and tatty shorts that are **de rigueur** at this level). We were spat at, kicked and punched. Protests were met with disdain and the threat of 'real' violence.

We've learnt our lesson. Now our ragbag of fatties, speccies, softies (leavened with the odd ex-Spanish League pro and several architects who once had trials for QPR – I kid you not) plays only other soft, speccy fatties. And we're quite good, actually. We mark, keep to our positions and yell 'make a run!' and 'use the channels!' and stuff – just like proper footballers. And all of us have been brutalised out of 'proper' football – left broken-legged on Hackney marshes or ambushed by beer-crate wielding cockernee monsters after a pub game. So none of us are willing to take it that seriously …

But occasionally, when the evenings lengthen and the weather improves, we'll be lured from the Astroturf and back into the park – the spiritual home

de rigueur: required

of all lousy footballers. And inevitably there will come an evening when Arsenal or Chelsea or Man Utd are on Sky and half the team fails to turn up. So we'll challenge another bunch of lads to a game (Armani mock-Crombies for goalposts). And there's our goalkeeper, Parapa the Rapper (so called because he's skinny, looks about 12 and has one of those daft hip-hop woolly hats permanently glued to his head) rolling on the floor in agony. And the big lad who's just 'done' him (no-one's fault, like, just one of those 70-30 balls that you have to go for) is laughing in your face as you suggest that he might want to go and see if the kid he's assaulted is OK …

Listen, I'm not saying that we're angels. Beautiful little Raphael, the ex-pro, has the annoying habit of leaving his heel up to catch opponents. The goal-hanging giant Johnny Cigarettes has elbows that always seem to be sticking out at head height. Matt the Ginger Rhino will invariably respond to any comment on his performance (even if favourable) with a torrent of gruff Humberside expletives. And Geordie Phil The Mad Communist Teacher has screamed himself into a froth of unintelligible hysterics by the end of every game. In fact, thinking about it, they're a bunch of brutes. But there's not a Park Football Psychopath among them. And once again my Sunday afternoons are very heaven.

Steven Wells, *FourFourTwo*, September 2001

Extract 1.7
George Orwell wrote essays and novels – including *Animal Farm* and *1984*. Although he was born to fairly wealthy parents and went to school at Eton, he soon left behind his rich background to earn his living as a writer. Here he describes his life in Paris and what happened when he began to run out of money.

Learning to be Poor

I lived in the Coq d'Or quarter for about a year and a half. One day, in summer, I found that I had just **four hundred and fifty francs** left, and beyond this nothing but thirty-six francs a week, which I earned by giving English lessons. I decided to start looking for a job, and – very luckily as it turned out – I took the precaution of paying two hundred francs for a month's rent in advance. With the other two hundred and fifty francs, besides the English lessons, I could live a month, and in a month I should probably find work. I aimed at becoming a guide to one of the tourist companies, or perhaps an interpreter. However, a piece of bad luck prevented this.

One day there turned up at the hotel a young Italian who called himself a **compositor**. Madame F. did not like the look of him, and made him pay a week's rent in advance. The Italian paid the rent and stayed six nights at the hotel. During this time he managed to prepare some duplicate keys, and on the last night he robbed a dozen rooms. Luckily he did not find the money that was in my

---

four hundred and fifty francs: roughly equivalent to £180 in today's money
compositor: typesetter for a printer

pockets, so I was not left penniless. I was left with just forty-seven francs – that is, **seven and ten-pence**.

This put an end to my plans of looking for work. I had now got to live at the rate of six francs a day, and from the start it was too difficult to leave much thought for anything else. It was now that my experience of poverty began – for six francs a day, if not actual poverty, is on the fringe of it. Six francs is **a shilling**, and you can live on a shilling a day in Paris if you know how. But it is a complicated business.

It is altogether curious, your first contact with poverty. You have thought so much about poverty – it is the thing you have feared all your life, the thing you knew would happen to you sooner or later; and it is all so utterly and **prosaically** different. You thought it would be quite simple; it is extraordinarily complicated. You thought it would be terrible; it is merely squalid and boring. It is the peculiar *lowness* of poverty that you discover first; the shifts that it puts you to, the complicated meanness, the crust-wiping.

You discover, for instance, the secrecy attaching to poverty. At a sudden stroke you have been reduced to an income of six francs a day. But of course you dare not admit it – you have got to pretend that you are living quite as usual. From the start it tangles you in a net of lies, and even with the lies you can hardly manage it. Meals are the worst difficulty of all. Every day at meal-times you go out, **ostensibly** to a restaurant, and loaf an hour in the Luxembourg Gardens, watching the pigeons. Afterwards you smuggle food home in your pockets. Your food is bread and margarine, or bread and wine, and even the

---

seven and ten-pence: roughly equivalent to £18.80 today
a shilling: worth roughly £1.00 today
prosaically: dully, boringly
ostensibly: apparently

nature of the food is governed by lies. You have to buy rye bread instead of household bread, because the rye loaves, though dearer, are round and can be smuggled in your pockets. This wastes you a franc a day. Your linen gets filthy, and you run out of soap and razor-blades. Your hair wants cutting, and you try to cut it yourself, with such fearful results that you have to go to the barber after all, and spend the equivalent of a day's food. All day you are telling lies, and expensive lies.

You discover what it is like to be hungry. With bread and margarine in your belly, you go out and look into the shop windows. Everywhere there is food insulting you in huge, wasteful piles; whole dead pigs, baskets of hot loaves, great yellow blocks of butter, strings of sausages, mountains of potatoes, vast Gruyère cheeses like grindstones. A snivelling self-pity comes over you at the sight of so much food. You plan to grab a loaf and run, swallowing it before they catch you; and you **refrain**, from pure **funk**.

You discover the boredom which is inseparable from poverty; the times when you have nothing to do and, being underfed, can interest yourself in nothing. For half a day at a time you lie on your bed. Only food could rouse you. You discover that a man who has gone even a week on bread and margarine is not a man any longer, only a belly with a few accessory organs.

This – one could describe it further, but it is all in the same style – is life on six francs a day. Thousands of people in Paris live it – struggling artists and students, prostitutes when their luck is out, out-of-work people of all kinds. It is the suburbs, as it were, of poverty.

I continued in this style for about three weeks.

These three weeks were squalid and uncomfortable, and evidently there was worse coming, for my rent would

---

refrain: hold back
funk: fear, cowardice

be due before long. Nevertheless, things were not a quarter as bad as I had expected. For, when you are approaching poverty, you make one discovery which outweighs some of the others. You discover boredom and mean complications and the beginnings of hunger, but you also discover the great redeeming feature of poverty: the fact that it **annihilates** the future. Within certain limits, it is actually true that the less money you have, the less you worry. When you have a hundred francs in the world you are liable to the most craven panics. When you have only three francs you are quite indifferent; for three francs will feed you till tomorrow, and you cannot think further than that. You are bored, but you are not afraid. You think vaguely, 'I shall be starving in a day or two – shocking, isn't it?' And then the mind wanders to other topics. A bread and margarine diet does, to some extent, provide its own **anodyne**.

And there is another feeling that is a great consolation in poverty. It is a feeling of relief, almost of pleasure, at knowing yourself at last genuinely down and out. You have talked so often of going to the dogs – and well, here are the dogs, and you have reached them, and you can stand it. It takes off a lot of anxiety.

George Orwell, *Orwell and the Dispossessed*

---

annihilates: destroys, does away with
anodyne: pain-killer

Extract 1.8
In this article, written for *Granta* magazine, Linda Grant explores her own feelings about her elderly mother when the two are out shopping. Something seems not quite right. What is it and how do we get to know?

Are We Related?

My mother and I are going shopping, as we have done all our lives. 'Now Mum,' I tell her, 'don't start looking at the prices on everything. I'm paying. If you see something you like, try it on. You are the mother of the bride, after all.' At long last one of her two daughters (not me) is getting married.

'So we're looking for a dress?' A nice dress. The sales are still raging through the summer's heat, hot shoppers toiling up and down Oxford Street. We should, I think, find something for £60 or £70. 'John Lewis is full of them,' a friend has said. She has an idea of the kind of dress someone's mother would wear, an old biddy's frock, a shapeless floral sack.

'I don't think that's her kind of thing,' I had told her, doubtfully. But then who knew what was left? Could my mother's fashion sense be so far eroded that she would have lost altogether those modes of judgement that saw that something was classic and something else was merely frumpy?

'I'm not having a dress, I want a suit,' my mother says as the doors part automatically to admit the three of us, for tagging along is my nephew, her grandson, who also likes to shop.

'OK. A suit. Whatever you like.'

And now we're in the department store, our idea of a second home.

And no outing can offer more escape from the nightmare of her present reality than shopping for clothes, the easiest means we know of becoming our fantasies and generally cheering ourselves up all round. Who needs the psychiatrist's couch when you have shopping? Who needs Prozac?

Up the escalators to the first floor where the land of dreams lies all around us, suits and dresses and coats and skirts and jackets. And where to begin? How to start? But my mother has started already.

At once a sale rack has caught her eye with three or four short navy wool crêpe jackets with nipped-in waists, the lapels and slanted pockets edged in white, three mock mother-of-pearl buttons to do it up. My mother says she thinks she is a size twelve. She tries the jacket on right then and there and it takes fifty years off her. She stands in front of the mirror as Forties Miss, dashing about London in the Blitz, on the way to her job in Top Ops. She turns to us, radiant. 'What do you think?'

'Perfect.' The sleeves are too long, but this is a small matter. We will summon the seamstress and she will take them up, her mouth full of pins. As my mother folds the sleeves under I steal a covert look at the price tag. The jacket is reduced to £49.99, and this, in anybody's book, is a bargain.

'Now I need a skirt and blouse. I've got to match the navy.'

She disappears between the rails and I am anxious for it is not hard to lose sight of her.

She's back quickly with her selection. The navy of the skirt and blouse she has chosen match each other and the jacket exactly, which isn't the easiest thing in the world to do so that I know that her perception of colour is quite unaltered and whatever else is wrong with her, there is nothing the matter with her eyes. I take the garments from her as we walk to the changing rooms, for everything apart from the smallest and lightest of handbags is too heavy for her now. A full mug of tea is too heavy for her to pick up. In cafes where they serve coffee in those large green and gold cups from France, she is **stymied**, remains thirsty.

What she gives me to hold is a Karl Lagerfeld skirt and a Jaeger blouse, both substantially reduced, at £89.99 and £69.99, but not within the £60 budget I had estimated when the old biddy dress came to mind, like those which hang from rails ignored by my mother. She has obeyed my instruction. She has not looked at the prices. Half-submerged in whatever part of the brain contains our capacity to make aesthetic judgements, her old good taste is buried and my injunction to ignore the prices has been the key that released it. A young woman of twenty-five could attend a job interview in the outfit she has put together.

In the changing room, she undresses.

The ensemble is in place when I look back. The pencil skirt, a size ten, is an exact fit but the blouse (also a ten) is a little too big, billowing round her hips, which is a shame for it is beautiful, in heavy matte silk with white overstitching along the button closings.

And now my mother turns to me in rage, no longer placid and obedient, not the sweet little old-age pensioner that shop assistants smile at to see her delight in her new jacket.

Fury devours her. 'I will not wear this blouse, you will not make me wear this blouse.' She bangs her fist against the wall and (she is the only person I have ever seen do this) she stamps her foot, just like a character from one of childhood comics or a bad actress in an amateur production.

---

stymied: stuck, baffled

'What's the matter with it?'

She points to the collar. 'I'm not having anyone see me in this. It shows up my neck.'

I understand for the first time why, on this warm July day as well as every other, she is wearing a scarf knotted beneath her chin. I had thought her old bones were cold, but it is vanity. My mother was seventy-eight the previous week. 'Go and see if they've got it in a smaller size,' she orders.

There is no size eight on the rack and I return empty-handed. My mother is standing in front of the mirror regarding herself: her fine grey hair, her hazel eyes, her obstinate chin, the illusory remains of girlish prettiness, not ruined or faded or decayed but withered. Some people never seem to look like grown-ups but retain their childish faces all their lives and just resemble elderly infants. My mother did become an adult once but then she went back to being young again; young with lines and grey hair. Yet when I look at her I don't see any of it. She's just my mother, unchanging, the person who tells you what to do.

'Where've you been?' she asks, turning to me. 'This blouse is too big round the neck. Go and see if they have it in a smaller size.'

'That's what I've been doing. They haven't.'

'Oh.'

So we continue to admire the skirt and the jacket and wait for the seamstress to arrive, shut up in our little cubicle where once, long ago, my mother would say to me: 'You're not having it and that's final. I wouldn't be seen dead with you wearing something like that. I don't care if it's all the rage. I don't care if everyone else has got one. You can't.'

My mother fingers the collar on the blouse. 'I'm not wearing this, you know. You can't make me wear it. I'm not going to the wedding if I've got to wear this blouse.'

'Nobody's going to make you wear it. We'll look for something else.'

'I've got an idea. Why don't you see if they have it in a smaller size.'

'I've looked already. There isn't one. This is the last . . .'

'No, I must interrupt you. I've just thought, do you think they've got it in a smaller size?'

'That's what I'm trying to tell you. They haven't got one.'

Her shoulders sag in disappointment. 'Anyway,' I say, to distract her, 'the seamstress will be along in a minute to take up the sleeves.'

She looks down at her arms. 'Why? They aren't too long.'

'That's because you folded them up.'

She holds the cuffs between her fingers. 'Oh, that's right.' She looks back at herself in the mirror, smiling. 'I love this jacket. But I don't like the blouse. Well, I do like it but it's too big round the neck. Why don't you nip outside and see if they've got a smaller one?'

'I've been. They haven't. I've told you already.'

'Did you? I don't remember. Have I ever told you that I've been diagnosed as having a memory loss?'

'Yes.'

Now the seamstress has come. My mother shows her the blouse. 'It's too big round the neck,' she tells her. 'Can you take it in?'

'No, Mum, she's here to alter the jacket.'

'Why? There's nothing the matter with it.'

'Yes there is. The sleeves are too long.'

'No they aren't.'

'That's because you've turned them up.'

'Well, never mind that. Go and see if they've got this blouse in a smaller size.'

And so it goes, like Alice in the garden, on the path where whatever she does always leads straight back to where she started. We are through the looking glass now, my mother and I, where we wander in that terrible wilderness without landmarks, nothing to tell you that you passed here only moments before.

We pay for the jacket and the skirt, leave John Lewis and walk a few yards to the next store which is D.H. Evans.

Up the escalator to the dress department and on a sale rack is the very Jaeger blouse! There are plenty of them and right at the front what is there but an eight.

'Look!' I cry. 'Look what they've got and in your size.'

My mother runs towards me, she really does pick up her legs and break into a trot. '*Well*, they didn't have that in John Lewis.'

'They did but it was too big and they didn't have a smaller one.'

'Did they? I don't remember.'

She tries the blouse on in the changing rooms. The fit is much better. She looks at the label. 'Jaguar. I've never heard of them.' Her eyes, which could match navy, sometimes jumbled up letters.

'Not jaguar, Jaeger.'

'Jaeger! I've never had Jaeger in my life before.'

'You must be joking. You've a wardrobe full of it.'

'Have I? I don't remember. Have I told you I've been diagnosed with a memory loss?'

'Yes,' I say. 'You've told me.'

'And now,' my mother announces, 'I need a jacket and a skirt.'

'We've bought those already.'

'Where are they then?'

'The skirt is in this bag and the jacket is being altered.'

'Are you sure?'

'Positive.'

'What colour are they?'

'Navy.'

'Well, that's lucky,' she says pointing triumphantly to the blouse, 'because this is navy.'

My mother wants to take the tube home (or rather to the Home in which we have **incarcerated** her) for a taxi is an unnecessary extravagance. 'I'm fresh,' she says. But I am not. A moment always comes, towards the end of these outings, when I want to go into a bar and have a drink, when I wish I carried a hip flask of innocuous vodka to sip, sip, sip at throughout the day. Most of all I want it to stop, our excursion. I can't put up with any more and I fall into cruel, monosyllabic communication. 'Yes, Mum.' 'No, Mum.' 'That's right.' 'Mmm.'

Here is a taxi and do not think for a moment, Madam, that despite the many burdens of your shopping, however swollen your feet or **fractious** your child, that you are going to take this cab before me.

'Get in,' I order. As we drive off up Portland Place I am calculating how much her old biddy outfit has cost. It has come to £209.97 which is more than I have paid for mine and has beaten out all of us, including the bride herself, on designer labels.

My mother holds on to her two purchases, from which floral prints have been rigorously excluded.

She looks at us both, her daughter and grandson. She's puzzled about something. She has a question she needs to ask. 'Just remind me,' she says. 'How am I related to you?'

Linda Grant, *Granta: The First Twenty-One Years* 1997

---

incarcerated: imprisoned
fractious: irritated, bad-tempered

Extract 1.9
Desmond Morris is a zoologist who spends much of his working life communicating his enthusiasm for animals through books and popular television programmes. Here he explores his early interest in animals and how it shaped his professional life.

The Animal-Watcher

As a boy one of my greatest pleasures was watching animals. I divided my time between my hundreds of pet animals at home and the wild animals in the Wiltshire countryside. I spent so much time with them that I began to think like them, to see the world from their point of view. I identified with them so strongly that I began to see humans who hunted animals as the enemy. At the time this was an unfashionable attitude. Hunting-shooting-and-fishing was the norm. In the British countryside where I wandered, everyone did it. It was a way of life. But from an early age, for some reason, I rebelled. I preferred foxes to foxhounds. I found wildfowl more fascinating than wildfowlers. And I hated the anglers with their sharp hooks and their lack of understanding of what they were doing to the fish they plucked so gleefully from their wet world into our dry one.

Above all, I wanted to understand the world of animals. There were so many mysteries and it was hard to know how or where to begin. I tried to get closer to them. I discovered that sitting very still for as long as possible was the first great secret. Most people, I noticed, even experienced naturalists, were forever striding through the undergrowth, striking out across the fields, and searching, searching for something new. Far better, it seemed to me, was the simple strategy of waiting for nature to come to you, rather than going clumsily to look for it.

When Picasso was asked how he painted, he replied, 'I do not seek, I find.' Already, in my childhood, this had become my way of studying animals. When you walk into a wood or a field, you alarm everything that lives there. The moving human body is large, obtrusive and highly visible. But sit down quietly and, after a while, you become invisible. Nature resumes its activities, the patterns of behaviour you disrupted by your arrival. This is true whether you are in a desert or a forest or swimming on a coral reef.

When I was still very young I built myself a raft from old planks and oil-drums. I launched it on to a small lake and, lying flat on its wooden platform, pressed my face close to the water. The raft drifted very slowly, making no disturbance, and there through the mirror-smooth surface I saw a giant pike, lying in wait for its prey like a lurking U-boat. A shoal of young roach approached it unawares, sensed its presence and immediately closed ranks – safety in numbers – before darting off. I was so close to the water that I was already beginning mentally to enter their world and to feel their dramas as my dramas.

This was all happening half a century ago, before the invention of the **aqualung**. But I was already close enough to the aquatic world for it to become a lifelong obsession. It did not replace my fascination for mammals, birds and reptiles. It simply gave my study another dimension. My appetite for learning about all animals, simple or complex, **was insatiable**. Inevitably I was destined to become a zoologist in later life.

---

aqualung: portable diving equipment, enabling divers to swim around freely underwater
was insatiable: could not be satisfied

The great problem I faced, when I eventually obtained my degree in zoology, was that to convert my childhood fascination into an adult career I would have to carry out experiments on animals. Zoology was in an intensely experimental, laboratory-oriented phase, and this did not appeal to me. I was simply not prepared to treat animals in that way. In my mind I was one of them and there was no way I was going to make a living from carrying out painful experiments on friends. It looked very much as though I would have to find some other career.

Just as I was about to give up zoology, I was lucky enough to attend a lecture by the great ethologist Niko Tinbergen. I had no idea what ethology was, but I soon found out. It was the naturalistic study of animal behaviour. Tinbergen demonstrated that it was possible, simply by watching animals, to make a scientific study of them. By making the watching systematic and analytical, it was possible to carry out field experiments that reduced interference with the animals to a minimum. He demonstrated that it was possible to convert amateur natural history into professional zoology by the straightforward device of **quantified observation**.

For me this was a revelation. It meant that, by carefully counting and scoring different animal actions in given time periods, I could make complicated analyses that helped to unravel the intricate behaviour patterns that existed in so many species. It meant that instead of guessing that the presence of a red spot or the flicking of a tail was acting as a threat signal or a courtship display, I could set about proving it. There was no looking back. A whole new world of animal study lay open to me and has continued to excite me ever since . . .

---

quantified observation: scientific observation based on noting down the quantity of particular actions or events

The serious student of animal behaviour starts out with a basic premise, namely that every spot of colour, every strange posture, every tiny movement that an animal makes, has some special meaning. Furthermore, all these colours and actions can be understood if they are studied closely enough. Nothing an animal ever does cannot be explained, given sufficient patience and ingenuity on the part of the animal-watcher. Everything has a reason, every piece of behaviour functions in some way to improve the chances of survival of the animal concerned. In the end, all animal mysteries can be unravelled.

To some romantics this may seem a pity. They would prefer to keep the mysteries of nature as mysterious as possible. They feel that to explain everything will be destroy the beauty of nature, but they are wrong. To know that a particular animal dance, or brightly coloured display, operates as a territorial device or as a sexual arousal mechanism does not make it any less beautiful. To understand the function of bird-song does not make it any less enchanting. The romantic refusal to analyse is based on a **fallacy**. It also introduces a dangerous bias. For, to the romantic, the bird of paradise is much more exciting than the humble house sparrow. Any animal species that happens to be superficially dull will be ignored, perhaps even maltreated. But to the ethologist, every species is fascinating – the end-point of millions of years of complex evolutionary pressures. Every species has its own intricate behaviour repertoire of survival mechanisms and even the seemingly boring species soon become exciting when one starts to probe into their particular way of life. The social behaviour of the despised house sparrow is every bit as intriguing as that of the bird of paradise to the serious animal-watcher.

---

fallacy: false idea, misunderstanding

A final comment on my use of the word 'animal'. Many people confuse the terms 'animal' and 'mammal'. They speak of fish and insects, for example, as though they were not animals. What they mean, of course, is that they are not mammals. All living things are either plants or animals. The amoeba is just as much an animal as the elephant. So animal-watching covers everything from microscopic creatures to mammalian giants. But, having said this, I must admit that I have favoured familiar species or, at least, species that are relatives of familiar species . . . We can learn more about ourselves from monkeys than from microbes, and looking around our modern human world it is clear that we need to discover as much as we can about ourselves.

As I have said before, when writing about human behaviour, we are no more than swollen-headed animals and the sooner we accept this fact the safer we will be. As risen apes we have come to dominate this small planet so effectively that we are in danger of smothering it. There are many lessons we can learn from other animals, to our great and continuing advantage, and it is high time we took a little while to sit and stare at the other creatures with which we share the earth. They have much to teach us.

Desmond Morris, *The Animal-Watcher*

Extract 1.10

Sue Sabbagh is a writer and journalist, and also the mother of three healthy and successful children. A fourth child, her first-born, died at the age of two months. Here Sue talks about her experiences and feelings during this intensely emotional period.

ONE IN A HUNDRED

People ask about Isabella: 'Is she your first baby?' It's simpler to answer, 'Yes,' but it's not the truth. Lucy was, and always will be, my first baby. People are embarrassed if I say I had a baby who died. They don't realize the memory of Lucy is a joy for me as well as a wound. I hate to deny her brief existence by pretending that my bouncing 14-month-old is my first.

Lucy was born three weeks prematurely in January 1970. I had been well and happy throughout my pregnancy, but one day I had a low dragging backache, and as I got into bed that evening I thought I felt the waters break. I mopped myself with a towel. It wasn't water, it was bright red blood and it went on flowing. Our doctor wasn't available. At last a deputizing doctor arrived and asked me a great many questions like what did my father do and had I had chicken pox? I was frightened by the blood I was losing, which of course wasn't really very much, but it felt like pints and I longed for him to do something. At last he explained that I had gone into labour and that the placenta was probably slightly misplaced so that the baby's head was pressing on it and causing the bleeding. He sent for an ambulance and I went into hospital.

My husband was away. My mother asked if she could stay with me. The night nurse was sharp. 'What for?' she said. After a bit she said, 'Yes, if you want,' but by then I had persuaded my mother to go. I was sure, I lied, that it would be all right. The sister came and gave me an injection. A few minutes later I felt very sick and rang to ask for a bowl. She was busy, could I wait a bit? I was humiliatingly sick on the sheet, which she insisted, crossly, on changing, though I suggested apologetically that she could just sponge it. I was clearly being a nuisance.

I went on having **ineffectual** and irregular contractions all that night and the next morning. It just felt like one long backache which never went away. People came and examined me. I was still losing blood. At about mid-day they decided to give me a general anaesthetic and see what was going on. When I came round, I asked quickly, 'Have they done a Caesarean?' I'd been warned they might have to, but no, they had just broken the waters. I would have the baby normally. I was delighted. I'd looked forward to helping my baby be born, and although

---

ineffectual: useless, unproductive

we'd been abroad and I hadn't been able to attend proper ante-natal classes, I'd studied **Erna Wright's** method of breathing and relaxation and tried to practise it on my own, with my husband's help. He was here now, having travelled all night. He held my hand and encouraged me marvellously. Towards the end of the first stage, I asked for the gas and air machine. It didn't seem to make any difference at all.

'I think perhaps the cylinder's empty,' I suggested nervously.

'Nice deep breaths, dear,' the midwife said.

After a while the day sister, the nice one who had smiled at me over her mask when I was being wheeled into the operating theatre earlier, came in and looked at the gas and air thing. 'This is empty,' she said, 'I'll get you another.'

Lucy was born at 8.30 p.m. She didn't cry or move much, and was having trouble with her breathing. I held her for minute or two (so warm and damp and crumpled). 'Hallo, what a funny little face you've got,' I said fondly. The words returned to haunt me later. They whisked her off to an **incubator**. Karl went home, very proud. I was stitched up and given tea, and wheeled back to sleep.

I woke early in the morning, still in the single ward, and asked the nurse who came to take away

---

Erna Wright: a promoter of natural childbirth
incubator: a special protective cradle for premature babies

the blood transfusion equipment how my daughter was. It was the sharp night sister again, but strangely softened. 'She went a bit blue in the night, dear,' she said, 'but she's nice and pink now.' I thought: 'Poor little girl's exhausted after her long drawn out entry into the world,' and I didn't worry at first that they didn't let me see her. The morning dragged on. Nobody came. I did my nails, and that was another little thing that hurt my conscience later. ('I did my nails, and all the time …') Then someone said something outside in the corridor and another voice hissed, 'Shh! She doesn't know anything about it yet,' and all of a sudden I was terrified. This was the nightmare of every pregnant woman come true. Something was wrong with Lucy. Perhaps she was dead. I rang frantically for a nurse. An old, deaf sister came and she couldn't hear my questions and she absolutely wouldn't tell me anything except that the **paediatrician** was coming to see me. It suddenly occurred to me that it was odd that Karl hadn't been in to see me yet. Apparently they wanted the paediatrician to talk to me first. Finally my frantic appeals induced the old nurse to reply tentatively, 'Well dear, they think there may be something wrong with baby's ears.' So that was it. She would be deaf. Dear God, and I had been inwardly

---

paediatrician: a doctor specialising in childhood illnesses

cursing this poor woman's deafness as though it were an irritating affectation.

At that moment Karl arrived, and with relief I begged him to tell me the truth. Was Lucy deaf? It was worse than that, he said, and he told me that Lucy was badly damaged. Her ears were slightly malformed, and they weren't sure whether she would be able to hear or see. She had severe brain damage. She couldn't breathe or swallow easily. They had rung him shortly after he got home last night and he had had all night and half a day to think about it, forbidden to come to me.

Before I had had time to **assimilate** anything of this, but had uttered one involuntary cry of pain, the paediatrician came briskly in and sat on my bed. He seized my hands extremely firmly and started saying, 'Now, now, now, now, now … you must be sensible. You must not reject that baby. That baby needs you. You mustn't think it's your fault.' He did not wish to waste time on emotion. He meant well, but his words bore little relation to my feelings, which although they contained shock, horror, disappointment, were chiefly a great surge of love and pity and a craving to hold my baby and reassure her and myself.

I was allowed to look at her in her incubator, through a window. She didn't look awful at all. Her

assimilate: take in, digest

little ears were pointed like a pixie's and she was very pale. She had quite a lot of soft, gold hair.

Lucy was christened in her incubator two days later and I was sent home. That was a dreadful moment, to carry a baby inside you and then have her separated from you by glass and corridors and roads and traffic.

The one **tenuous** link I had with her was almost denied me. A nurse had come to give me some pills that first, numb evening. Luckily, I had asked what they were for. 'To dry up your milk,' she said.

'But I want to feed her!'

'The baby won't be able to suck, dear,' she told me.

No, but I could, and did, express milk for her. Once they had got over their surprise, the nurses were very encouraging, and soon I was proudly taking in 24 oz or more every day. It was far more than Lucy needed, so they asked me if they could give some of it to another, even tinier **prem**. baby. The paediatrician wrote to me a year or two later, with a photo of this boy, now a sturdy little chap, thanking me for helping to save his life. None of the other mothers on the ward had wanted to breast-feed.

Giving my milk helped immeasurably to ease the dreadful frustration of my maternal longing, and of

---

tenuous: thin, fragile
prem.: premature, born early

course it helped Lucy too. She put on a little weight and was able to leave the incubator. I could hold her. I even bathed her, with Karl taking photographs.

Our GP, a kind man, felt I was 'getting too obsessed with this milk business'. He suggested I pack it in, and start going out to dinner and thinking about other things. He meant well, but again I felt that nobody understood. In the end I had to stop because they moved Lucy to a hospital much further away to do all sorts of tests on her. They thought her chromosomes might be abnormal. The tests showed her condition wasn't hereditary. The genetic damage had been done by a uterine infection.

Lucy was a real fighter, everyone admired her spirit, but after eight battling weeks she had had enough. The sister rang me very early one morning. They thought there was a change in her condition. There had been a time like this before when I had sat by her cot, holding her hand and pleading with her to hang on. That time she had, but this time as soon as I saw her exhausted face and heard the infinitely laboured breathing I knew she couldn't live. She was propped up in the cot, and I held the oxygen mask for her and stroked her hair. It was misty and quiet outside with birds singing. She turned towards me and then she turned towards the window and her eyes filled with light and she died.

She taught me how to die, and she convinced me that death is not the end. Lucy is still my first child, and I remember her, after the pain, with joy.

Sue Sabbagh, *World Medicine*, April 1974

Extract 1.11

On 6 August 1945, towards the end of the Second World War, the American Air Force dropped two atomic bombs on the Japanese cities of Hiroshima and Nagasaki. Nobody had used atomic bombs before, and no one knew quite what to expect – least of all the civilians who were caught in the explosions. This is part of the diary of one woman who was in Hiroshima when the bomb fell.

City of Corpses

The air raid alarm sounded in Hiroshima and the neighbourhood group sent round a warning to be ready to flee at any moment. So on the night of the fifth, sleep was wholly out of the question.

At daybreak the air raid alarm was lifted; shortly after seven the alert too was lifted. I went back to bed. I usually slept late anyway, and since I had just been discharged from the hospital, where I often slept till almost noon, I was left alone until the bright light flashed.

I was sound asleep inside the mosquito net. Some say it was 8:10 when the bomb fell; some say 8:30. Whichever it was, I dreamed I was enveloped by a blue flash, like lightning at the bottom of the sea. Immediately thereafter came a terrible sound, loud enough to shake the earth. With an indescribable sound, almost like a roll of thunder, like a huge boulder tumbling down a mountain, the roof of the house came crashing down. When I came to, I was standing there, dazed, in a cloud of dust – the plaster walls smashed to smithereens. I was standing there completely in a fog, struck absolutely dumb. I felt no pain; I was not frightened; I was somehow calm and vaguely light-headed. The sun, which had shone so brightly early that morning, had faded, and the light was dim, almost as in the evening during the rainy season.

On the second floor I could see nothing at all. The only thing left was a small pile of dirt, dust rising from it, glass broken into tiny fragments, and a small mound of pieces of roof tile; of the mosquito net and even of the bed, there was not the slightest trace. There were none of the things that had been at my bedside: no **flak jacket**, no helmet, no watch, no books. Inside the house there was nothing at all to be seen. But outside, as far

---

flak jacket: a protective jacket to shield the wearer from bomb fragments

as the eye could see – which was much farther than usual – there stretched ruined house after ruined house. The same was true even of those parts of town a long way off.

In the case of the house across the street, only the stone gate remained, standing all by itself; the house had collapsed utterly and completely. In the gate a young girl was standing dazedly, as if stripped of all life. She looked up at me, in full view on the second floor, and said, 'Oh!' Then, in a subdued voice: 'Climb down quickly!' I could not climb down. Both stairways, front and back, were still standing, unbroken; but they were blocked halfway up by boards and tiles and dirt, a pile taller than I.

I had the girl from the house in front summon someone from my family. I counted on them, yet I felt they would never come.

Smeared with blood, her face transformed monstrously, Sister came climbing halfway up the stairs. As if she had dyed it, her white dress had become pure red; her jaw was wrapped in a white cloth, and her face was already swollen up like a pumpkin.

My first question: 'Is Mother alive?'

'Yeah, she's okay. She's watching you from the cemetery out back. The baby's alive, too. Quick, come on down.'

'How'm I going to get down? It looks impossible.' Relieved that Mother was alive, I found my strength had deserted me. With both hands, Sister pushed away at the stuff obstructing the staircase. Then she closed her eyes tight and looked about to collapse on top of the pile. Looking at her, I said, 'Please go back. I'll be right down.'

She replied: 'You're not so badly injured as I am, so do get yourself out somehow!' As she said this, I noticed for the first time that the collar of my **kimono** was thoroughly drenched in blood. As I left the room, this room I would never enter again, this room that had been home to me these several months, I took a last look around. I couldn't see even a single handkerchief; where I thought the bed had been, I finally made out the Singer sewing machine, on its side and in pieces.

On the stairs, I opened a hole in the pile of debris just big enough to crawl through and

---

kimono: a wide-sleeved Japanese robe

went downstairs. The ground floor wasn't as much of a shambles as the second floor; the chests and trunks and boxes that Sister had packed just two days ago to take with her when she left for the countryside were piled impossibly on top of each other. In the garden behind the house, my large trunk and Mother's wicker trunk were half-buried, as if they had been hurled down with great force. Last night we had set them out on the edge of the second-floor balcony. If a **firebomb** attack came, we had planned to throw them down into the cemetery out back.

I joined Mother and Sister in the cemetery.

Where we were, things were quiet, hushed. (The newspaper wrote that there was 'instant pandemonium', but that was a preconceived notion on the part of the writer. In fact, an eerie stillness settled, so still that one wondered whether people, trees and plants hadn't all died at one fell swoop.) My mother said, 'we called up to you many times; didn't you hear us? We heard a scream; but then, no matter how many times we called, there was no answer. We figured you must be dead.' I couldn't

---

firebomb: incendiary bombs that spread blazing fires where they fell

remember having cried out. Mother went on: 'Was I happy when I looked from the cemetery and you were standing there staring!'

'Really?' I replied. 'We were lucky, weren't we! All of us survived.'

Seated on a gravestone, her face in her hands, Sister was barely staving off collapse. Mother handed the sleeping baby to me. To get water, Mother went back into the house, which looked as if it might collapse at any moment. She appeared to shrink as she walked through our house, through the house in front, too, and finally out the other side.

People from the house next door and from other houses in the neighbourhood gathered in the cemetery; most of them were barefoot, and every single one was drenched in blood. Heavily wooded, the cemetery was a large and pleasant space; curiously, not a single gravestone had been knocked over. Everyone was strangely calm. Their faces were calm and expressionless, and they talked among themselves exactly as they always did – 'Did you all get out?', 'You were lucky you weren't hurt badly', and so on. No one spoke of bombs or firebombs; they kept their mouths shut about such matters almost as if they thought them not proper subjects for Japanese to talk about.

As if creeping along the ground, thin smoke started to issue from the eastern part of the flattened neighbourhood. The trunk and the wicker suitcase were partly buried in the ground; intending to stow them in the air raid shelter I set my hand to them. But I was too weak. And if I gave the baby to Sister to hold, the baby would become covered with blood. So I gave up on the luggage.

Mother, who was not bleeding, had brought some cotton trousers for me, and I pulled them on. Then I put on some old straw sandals we used for going out into the fields and shouldered my satchel.

By the time we got out on to the road in front of the shrine, fire was already crawling towards us from across the road on the right. Nearby on the left the embankment was visible, and we saw five or six people walking along the railway tracks on top. Those people didn't seem to be in a rush; seeing this, we figured the fire couldn't be all that fierce yet.

Even though we were walking through a neighbourhood that had been demolished, it aroused no feeling in us at all. As if it were an everyday time and an ordinary occurrence, we did not feel surprise, we did not cry; so it was without particularly hurrying that we followed the others up on to the nearby embankment. On one side of the embankment was a quarter of government-owned homes for officials. But here, too, it was hushed and quiet; nowhere was anyone to be seen.

Each of the beautiful estates on the embankment had stone steps leading down from back garden to riverbed, so one could climb down. On the parts of the riverbed where water did not flow, there were vegetable gardens. Hedges formed boundaries between plots. It was to this riverbed that we climbed down from the demolished houses. (From our house to the riverbed was about three blocks. Probably a good forty minutes had elapsed since the bomb fell – as we sat disoriented in the cemetery and then came to the riverbed. But it was only long afterward that I managed to call to mind what had gone on during that time.)

The stream of people fleeing became constant and unending. Every last person who flocked to the riverbed had been injured. One might have thought the riverbed was open only to the injured. From the faces, hands, legs protruding from their clothing, it was impossible to tell what it was that had given these people their lacerations. But they had a half dozen or more cuts, and they were covered with blood.

Some people had many streaks of clotted blood on their faces and limbs, the blood already dried. Some were still bleeding; their faces, hands and legs were dripping blood. By now, all the faces, too, had been hideously transformed. The number of people on the riverbed increased every moment, and we began to notice people with severe burns. At first, we didn't realize their injuries were burns. There was no fire, so where and how could these people have got burned so badly? Strange, grotesque, they were pathetic and pitiable rather than frightening. They had all been burned in precisely the same way ... Normal burns are part red and part white, but these burns were ash-coloured. It was as if the skin

had been broiled rather than burned: ash-
coloured skin hung from their bodies, peeling off in
strips, like the skins of roast potatoes.

Virtually everyone was naked to the waist.
Their trousers were all tattered, and some people
were wearing only underpants. Their bodies were
distended, like the bodies of people who have
drowned. Their faces were fat and enormously
puffed up. Their eyes were swollen shut, and the
skin around their eyes was crinkly and pink. They
held their puffy swollen arms, bent at the elbows,
in front of them, much like crabs with their two
claws. And hanging down from both arms like rags
was grey-coloured skin. On their heads they
appeared to be wearing bowls: the black hair on
top was still there, having been protected by
their caps; but from the ears down, the hair had
disappeared, leaving a dividing line as sharp as if
the hair had been shaved off.

The fires spread fiercely, with irresistible
force. Close by on the right, flames even began to
spurt from the engine of the freight train
stopped in the very middle of the railway bridge.
One after the other, the black cars of the train

burst into flame, and when the fire got to the last
car, it sent sparks flying and belched thick smoke,
as if it had had a full load of gunpowder. It spat
fire; it was as if molten iron were gushing out of a
tunnel. Underneath the bridge, we could see over
there the shore of the elegant park; on the bank
there, too, demonic deep red flames crawled. Soon
the riverside began to burn, and we could see
groups of people crossing to the other side. The
river was burning fiercely. The people around us
on the riverbed attempted to flee upstream. Over
our heads, without letup, circling B-29s roared, a
sound we had grown accustomed to hearing; at
any moment strafing firebombs or bombs might
pour down on our miserable group.

People felt certain that there would be a
second wave to the attack. In one corner of my
heart, I thought: there's probably no need to
drop anything more.

While we hid in the grass or squatted beside
the river, fearing that we would be **strafed**, up
in the sky they were taking photographs. Out
in the open as we were, we had our pictures

---

strafed: hit by machine-gun fire from low-flying planes

taken from overhead, as did the entire devastated city.

A typhoon-like wind had arisen. Only its secondary gusts blew towards us, and soon large drops of rain fell. When Osaka burned, too, a wind arose, and rain fell; people emerged from their shelters carrying umbrellas even though the sun was shining. I had heard about that, so I opened the blue umbrella. The rain was blackish in colour. Countless sparks rained down in its midst.

I say sparks, and I thought they were small sparks; but these sparks were bits of rag and scraps of wood glowing bright red as they were swept along by the high wind. The sky became darker still, as if night had come, and the red ball of the sun seemed to sink rapidly out of a mass of black clouds.

The fires swelled, became mountainous, burned everything in their path, and proceeded on their way; the city was being destroyed a block at a time. The heat was unbearable. We could see the fires spreading to distant neighbourhoods and hear fiery explosions somewhere or other continually. No Japanese plane showed itself in the sky.

We could not conceive of the day's events being related in any way to the war. We had been flattened by a force – arbitrary and violent – that wasn't war. Moreover, fellow countrymen did not particularly encourage one another, nor did they console one another. They behaved submissively and said not a word. No one showed up to tend the injured; no one came to tell us how or where to pass the night. We were simply on our own.

Night fell. It was impossible to say just when. The day, too, had been dark, so between day and night there was no clear break.

Sister and I removed the kerchiefs that had protected our necks and faces all day long. For the first time we each got a good look at the other's angry-looking face, but we were beyond smiling at each other.

Neither of us could see her own face, but looking at the other's gave us a sense of the shape we were in. Sister's face was puffed up like a round loaf of bread, and her eyes, normally large, black and uncannily clear, had become mere slits; the skin around them looked as if dark ink had been spilt on it. A cut in the shape of a cross extended from the right edge of her lip to her cheek, so her whole mouth was twisted into a sideways and inverted letter L; it was so ugly I couldn't look at it for long. Her hair was caked with blood and with the red clay of the walls; she looked like a long-time beggar woman. Both Sister and I had bound up our wounds with strange material. Each of us had wrapped the cloth under her chin and tied it in a bow on top of her head. I had a deep cut from the middle of my left ear to down below the ear.

In the distance the fires still soared into the sky, burning fiercely. In the night Hakushima dimmed to the colour of ash. On the riverbank opposite, two or three houses still burned away, out of control. The flames burned wildly writhing and turning like giant snakes. The area over toward Ushita had already been on fire during the day; when night came, the fires burned from peak to peak on the low, wavy range; they looked like lights in a far-off town. Like shooting stars,

flames often flew across one peak and the next,
and then the second peak too caught fire. After
night fell, groaning voices, slow and dull, could be
heard coming from a distance. Monotonous
groaning voices, deeply melancholic, sounded here
and there.

   We lay down. Thanks to the forest fires and
the fires along the coast, it was bright and warm.
We listened to the groaning voices audible far and
near, as if to the sad sound of musical instruments.
The voices of insects, too, came to our ears. It
was all so very sad.

Ōta Yoko, *City of Corpses*

Extract 1.12

Jan Morris, a writer and journalist, gives an entertaining view of London as a city of theatre shows and tourist attractions – with the Queen as the biggest attraction of them all.

London: the City-Stage

One of the flight paths to London Airport, Heathrow, goes straight over the middle of the capital, east to west. The city does not look much at first: just a drab sprawling mass of housing estates, terraces and industrial plants, nibbled at its edges by a fairly grubby green – just mile after mile of the ordinary, splodged here and there with the sordid.

Presently, though, the route picks up the River Thames, **sinuously** sliding between the eastern suburbs, and one by one landmarks appear that are part of the whole world's consciousness, images familiar to every one of us, reflecting the experience of half mankind. The Tower of London squats brownish at the water's edge. Buckingham Palace reclines in its great green garden. The Houses of Parliament, of all famous buildings the most toylike and intricate, stand like an instructional model beside Westminster Bridge. There are the swathes of London parks, too, and the huge Victorian roofs of the railway terminals, the cluttered hub of Piccadilly, the big new block of Scotland Yard, and always the river itself, twisting and turning through it all, out of the city centre into the western **purlieus**, until the first country green appears on the other side, with gravel pits and motorways. Windsor

---

sinuously: moving like a snake
purlieus: districts, neighbourhoods

Castle appears tremendous on its hillock, and the aircraft, slightly changing its tone of voice, tilts a wing over Slough and begins the last descent to the airport.

It is the city of cities that we have flown over. Like it or loathe it, it is the daddy of them all . . . It has been itself, for better or worse, for a thousand years, unconquered by a foreign army since William the Norman was crowned King of England in Westminster Abbey in 1066. It has spawned and abandoned the greatest empire known to history. It was the first great industrial capital, the first parliamentary capital, the arena of social and political experiments beyond number.

Mozart wrote his first symphony in London, and Karl Marx began *Das Kapital*. London has five great symphony orchestras, eleven daily newspapers, three cathedrals, the biggest subway on earth and the most celebrated broadcasting system. It is the original world capital of soccer, cricket, rugby, lawn tennis and squash. It is where Jack the Ripper worked. It is the home of the last great monarchy of all, the House of Windsor. London is nearly everything. If you are tired of London, Dr Johnson once remarked, you are tired of life.

It is a gift of London, or rather a technique, that through the dingy and the disagreeable, the fantastic habitually looms. Illusion breaks in! Its principal agency is that monarchy whose heraldic lions, unicorns, crowns, roses, thistles and Norman mottoes are inescapable in this city . . .

The world flocks in to witness the mystery of London, enacted several times a year in the ceremonial thoroughfare called the Mall. The sidewalks then are thick with foreigners, and far away up Constitution Hill the tourist buses, emblazoned with the emblems and registration plates of all Europe, stand nose to nose in their shiny hundreds . . .

The beat of a drum is the start of the ritual, somewhere up there in the blur of gold, gray and green that is

Buckingham Palace. The beat of a drum, the blare of a band, and presently a procession approaches slowly between the plane trees. A drum major leads, in a peaked jockey cap and gilded tunic, **impassive** on his tall white horse. Then the jangling, clopping, creaking, panting cavalry, black horses, brass helmets, plumes, anxious young faces beneath their heavy helmet straps, the skid and spark of hoofs now and then, the shine of massive breastplates, sour smells of horse and leather. Three strange old gentlemen follow, weighed down beneath fat bearskin hats, with huge swords bouncing at their sides; they ride their chargers rheumatically stooped, as though they have been bent in the saddle like old leather.

Another plumed squadron . . . a pause . . . a hush over the crowd . . . and then, bobbing high above the people, almost on a level with the flags, the familiar strained and earnest face of the mystery itself, pale beneath its heavy makeup . . .

The Queen bobs away with her guards, her captains and her bands towards whatever elaborate and long, meaningless ceremonial has been prepared for her beyond the trees, but she leaves behind something stale . . . London seems often to be labouring beneath the weight of its own heritage – year after year, century upon century, the same beat of the drum major's drum, the same jangle of the harnesses, the same bent old courtiers on their chargers lurching generation after generation down the Mall.

Jan Morris, *Destinations: Essays from Rolling Stone*

---

impassive: showing no emotion

Activities

Writing to entertain

1   Before you start to read extracts from the above list, complete the following exercises.

   a   Write three or four sentences describing your bedroom as factually and accurately as possible.

   b   Now add adjectives and adverbs to make your bedroom sound:

      (i) warm and welcoming
      (ii) cold and frightening.

2   a   As you read the extracts from the above list, make notes on the authors' points of view towards the places or experiences they are describing. In particular, pick out and note down adjectives, adverbs and verbs that seem to you to be particularly interesting or effective in making the subject come alive for the reader.

   b   When you have finished reading, compare and discuss your findings with a partner or in a small group. Make notes of your findings.

   c   On your own or with a partner, select one of the extracts that you have read, then write two or three sentences stating the author's point of view towards his or her subject, giving evidence from the extract to back up your statement.

3 After reading and studying some or all of these extracts, think of a family occasion that you remember (for example, a birthday party, Christmas or a family celebration), then write an entertaining account of what happened. In your writing, you must:

   • address the reader directly
   • use adjectives and adverbs to make the occasion come alive for the reader.

Writing to explore

1 Before you start to read extracts from the above list, complete the following exercises.

   a Read the passage below, which tells part of the story of Little Red Riding Hood. All the verbs in the story are in the present tense. As you read, note down each verb as you come to it.

   > *Little Red Riding Hood puts on her cloak, picks up the pie and sets off through the wood to see her grandmother. The wolf watches from behind a tree and licks his lips. After watching carefully to see which way Little Red Riding Hood is going, the wolf sets off at a run, and races along a short-cut to Grandmother's house.*

b Re-write this passage, putting all the verbs in the past tense.

c In the passage below, the linking words that tell you *when* each action happened have been taken out and listed underneath. Copy the passage out, putting the linking words into their correct places.

_____ Melanie was cooking. Omar started laying the table. _____ he was putting a vase of flowers in the middle of the table, the cat came flying in. She was quickly followed by next door's dog. _____ Omar could do anything, the cat leaped on to the table and the vase crashed to the floor, splashing Omar, the cat and the dog with icy water, and flowers were scattered from one end of the room to the other. _____ a pause, _____ they all looked at each other, each of them fled in different directions. _____ Omar staggered, drenched, into the kitchen, the cat dived under the sofa, and the dog ran off into the garden. _____ one look at the mess in the dining room, Melanie and Omar decided to eat out.

after	after	as
before	during	while
while		

2 a As you read the extracts listed on page 67, notice the feelings of the writers towards the experiences they are describing.

b With a partner or in a small group, select one extract you have all read. Discuss what the writer was feeling. Note down evidence from the text to back your interpretation.

c On your own, write a short account of a personal experience that has helped you to understand what the writer of this extract was feeling. Begin your account with:

I can understand something of what the writer was feeling because I . . .

3 After reading and studying some or all of the extracts listed on page 67, choose an experience from your own life that you remember particularly vividly. Give a short account of your experience, exploring how you felt and why. In your account you must:

- set the events clearly in order
- make your feelings clear to the reader.

Writing to explore and entertain

1 Before you start to read extracts from the above list, complete the following exercises.

a Read through the five sentences that follow and note down the similes and metaphors used, saying which is which.

- Beckham streaked like lightning across the pitch.
- When Charlene saw the teacher, her heart sank like lead.
- Hassan hared across the road.
- The netball team blossomed under the new coach.
- His granny always said he was as sharp as a knife.

b Make up a sentence for each of the words
below, using either a metaphor or a simile in
your sentence. The first one has been done for
you.

sun	boy	girl
rain	dinosaur	mouse

The sun shone <u>like gold</u> across the river.

2 **a** As you read the extracts listed on page 69,
make notes of any details that help you to get a
picture of the people and places being
described.

b With a partner or in a small group, pool your
findings and draw up a final list of all the details
you have found.

c On your own, draw *either* three or four of the
people described in the extracts you have
already read *or* a plan of the place described in
one of the extracts. Label your drawing from
your list of details.

3 After reading and studying some or all of the
extracts listed on page 69, write about an event
that you have enjoyed. In your account you must:

• use the past tense
• use metaphors and similes to bring the event
alive for your reader.

Section 2

Writing to inform, explain, describe

The writers in this section can all be seen as being something of an authority on their subject matter. They all have knowledge they want to communicate to their readers, but they are doing it from slightly different standpoints, with slightly different purposes in mind.

Some of the writers in this section are writing purely to inform their readers about a topic. It is as if they are saying, 'I know about this topic; let me tell you about it.' Others, though, are seeking to go deeper into things, and to explain why the subject they are writing about is the way it is. They are saying, 'I know about this, and I can help you understand it.' The third group of writers in this section is trying to describe to their readers a sense of what their subject is really like: 'I know about this, and I can help you to feel what it is like and to experience it in the same way I did.'

Extract 2.1
This extract is taken from a biography of David Beckham.
The book charts David's route to fame from his early days
in football through to playing for the national squad and
how he became equally famous for marrying one of the
Spice Girls.

David Beckham –
Football, Fame and Fortune

Childhood
David Robert Joseph Beckham was born in London on 2
May 1975. He grew up in Leytonstone, in the East End. He
went to Chase Lane Juniors and Chingford High School.
David Beckham was never very good at school-work. He
just wanted to be a footballer . . .

When David Beckham was eight he played for Ridgeway
Rovers. They were good. They once won 23–0! He also
played for Waltham Forest and for Essex schoolboys. The
local paper called him the 'Chingford football sensation'.

When David Beckham was eleven he entered a
competition. It was run by Bobby Charlton's Coaching
School. Kids from all over the country took part. To win
you needed good ball control. David Beckham reached
the final. Guess where it was? Old Trafford!

Signing on
London clubs soon heard about the boy wonder. He had
trials with Spurs and Leyton Orient. Spurs wanted to sign
him. But David Beckham only wanted to play for
Manchester United.

One day he was playing for Waltham Forest. A scout
from Manchester United saw the game. United asked him

for a trial. They liked what they saw. On 2 May 1991 Alex Ferguson signed him for United. It was David Beckham's sixteenth birthday.

First team football
In October 1992 David Beckham played in the first team. He came on as a substitute against Brighton in the League Cup. He was just seventeen.

The next season he did not play for the first team at all – just for the Reserves. That season Manchester United won the Reserves' League.

Alex Ferguson wanted to give his young players first-team football. David Beckham went on loan to Preston North End. He played only four games for Preston but he scored twice. He was Man of the Match three times.

Number 7
David Beckham was soon a regular in the Manchester United first team. He played right midfield and scored eight goals in his first full season. He scored against Chelsea in the FA Cup semi-final. In the Cup Final Cantona scored the winning goal from a Beckham cross. That season Manchester United won the Double.

The next season United were Champions again. David Beckham scored twelve goals. He scored his most famous goal against Wimbledon. The Wimbledon keeper was off his line. David Beckham tried a shot from the half-way line. It went in!

At the end of the season Eric Cantona retired. Who was going to wear his Number 7 shirt? David Beckham. That season he scored eleven goals and he only missed one league game.

England
In 1996 England had a new manager. His name was Glen Hoddle. Hoddle wanted David Beckham to play for England.

David Beckham played in all the qualifying matches. Once he was booked for not getting on to a stretcher.

In 1998 David Beckham was picked to go to France for the World Cup.

He played as a wing-back against Tunisia. England won 2–0. He played in midfield against Colombia. David Beckham took a free kick. He curled the ball around the wall. It beat the Colombian keeper. It was a fantastic goal! England won 2–0. David Beckham was a national hero!

In the next round England played Argentina. After only six minutes Argentina were given a penalty. Battistuta scored. A few minutes later England were given a penalty. Alan Shearer scored. Then Michael Owen scored for England. It looked like England were going to win the game. Then disaster struck.

Diego Simeone tackled David Beckham. It was a bad tackle. David Beckham went down. David Beckham kicked Simeone. The referee saw it. He brought out a red card. David Beckham was sent off.

He had never been sent off before. Argentina soon scored again. England were knocked out on penalties.

All the English fans were very upset. Some fans were angry. Some fans blamed David Beckham.

They forgot his brilliant goal against Colombia.

Fame
It's hard being famous.

In 1997 David Beckham met Victoria Adams. She is one of the Spice Girls – better known as Posh Spice. He saw her on a Spice Girl video. Guess where they first met? That's right. Old Trafford!

It was love at first sight. They tried to keep it secret. But the press soon found out. Newspaper and television reporters followed them everywhere. They still do . . .

In July 1999 Victoria and David were married. The wedding was held in a castle in Ireland. There was a firework display, and an orchestra playing Spice Girl hits. The Spice Girls were there. All the Manchester United players were there. Gary Neville was the best man. Even the priest wore Manchester United socks!

Fortune

David Beckham plays for the biggest football club in the world. He plays for his country and scores amazing goals. He is the best crosser in the game and the highest-paid footballer in Britain.

His goal against Spurs brought the title back to Manchester United in 1999. It was their fifth title in seven years. That season they won the Treble. They won the Championship, the FA Cup and the European Champions' League.

David Beckham drives a Porsche. He models clothes. He is married to a pop-star. His favourite food is sticky toffee pudding and butterscotch sauce.

He is handsome, talented, famous, lucky, successful and very, very rich. What's more, he's still only in his twenties.

Some people think he is a hero. Some people don't like him. Some people envy him.

But everyone agrees, David Beckham is a brilliant footballer.

Andy Croft, *David Beckham*

Extract 2.2

In this extract, taken from her book on cats and cat care, Amanda Edwards explains how to look after a cat if it becomes ill or has an accident. As you read it, look at how she sets out the information so that it is clear and easy to understand.

First Aid For Your Cat

CONSTIPATION If you notice your cat straining to eject a motion, it could be that it is suffering from constipation. Elderly cats suffer more and fur balls can increase the problem. Feed fish in oil and add a little butter to help the passage of food through the cat's system. If after 24 hours the cat's bowels have still not moved, take it to the vet who may administer an **enema**. In the event of a cat being unable to urinate, this should be treated as an emergency.

ACCIDENTAL INJURY Cats are inquisitive animals and often have accidents. It is therefore essential that all cat owners are well prepared in the event of an emergency. If your cat is injured, try to keep calm, as it is essential that you focus your attention on saving your cat's life. If unsure what to do, immediately telephone your vet who may be able to give you life-saving advice. Exercise caution, as an animal that is injured or in distress

enema: a liquid or gas introduced into the rectum to ease constipation

is likely to scratch or bite its handler. Your two priorities should be to arrest any bleeding and maintain an airway. Only when you are sure that your cat is in a stable condition should you drive it to the veterinary hospital, which hopefully will have been pre-warned of your arrival. If possible, seek the help of a friend who can hold the injured animal in a blanket, keeping it quiet and warm until you arrive at your destination.

HOW TO RESUSCITATE YOUR CAT

Should your cat stop breathing for any reason, follow this procedure. It could save its life.

1 Lay your cat on its side on a blanket.
2 Open its mouth and make sure that the tongue is not obstructing the airways.
3 Tilt the cat's head back and hold the mouth shut. Blow into the nostrils for two or three seconds. Wait for the air to be expelled and then repeat until the cat starts to breathe.
4 If breathing fails to recommence after two or three minutes, lay the cat on its right side and firmly massage the area behind the shoulder, one hand resting on top of the other. Once the cat is breathing again, or if resuscitation fails, wrap it in a blanket and rush it to the vet. It will also help the vet if you can tell him what you think caused unconsciousness in the first place.

BITES Bite wounds are very common in cats, especially in those allowed to roam freely. While they are not usually serious in themselves, once a wound becomes infected or develops into an **abscess** it becomes more of a problem. Once a bite is discovered it is important to bathe it regularly in salty water to minimize the possibility of infection. Use a teaspoonful of salt in about half a pint of water. As a further precaution, consult your vet who is likely to prescribe antibiotics.

In a wound which has gone unnoticed, a painful abscess might well form, causing pain and a high temperature. It is important to take the cat to the vet immediately, who will drain the abscess and prescribe antibiotics.

BURNS If your cat is burnt, whether by scalding, a contact burn or by a **caustic substance**, it is important that you hold the affected part under running water for several minutes before seeking immediate veterinary advice. Never apply lotions, creams or butter or interfere with a burn in any other way as this worsens matters considerably and may cause infection.

CHOKING If your cat is in obvious distress, pawing at its mouth or straining in an attempt to

abscess: a collection of pus causing a swelling over an infected area
caustic substance: burning or corrosive substance, such as acid or bleach

vomit, it may be that it is choking. Restrain the cat immediately (using a towel), open up the mouth, and attempt to remove the offending object with tweezers. If you are unable to see the obstruction, seek immediate veterinary advice.

DROWNING It is very rarely that a cat will drown, possibly because they tend to avoid water at all costs; however, just once, the lure of a fish may prove too strong. Once a cat has fallen into a pond or river there is the danger that its lungs will rapidly fill with water, causing it to lose consciousness. If this occurs, hold the cat upside-down by its back legs and swing it gently in front of you and back between your legs, avoiding letting it touch the ground. This will usually expel the water from the lungs. If the cat still shows no sign of breathing, open its mouth, making sure the tongue is not obstructing the airways, and make an attempt to resuscitate it using the method above. Seek veterinary advice as soon as possible.

FALLS Cats love to climb and view the world from a high vantage point. They also seek refuge up trees when chased by dogs or when they have been frightened. Contrary to popular belief, cats do not always land on their feet and injuries from falls are commonplace. Fractures and other injuries to jaw and limbs are typical and cat owners should also be aware of concussion and the less obvious internal injuries which can occur.

If you should witness a cat's fall or suspect that it may have fallen, move it as little as possible and seek immediate veterinary advice.

ELECTRIC SHOCK These days, the large range of electrical appliances in every home presents an ever-present danger to cats, who appear to like chewing things. In the event of electric shock, switch off and disconnect the power supply before touching the cat or you will also endanger yourself. Use the resuscitation technique above to try to revive your pet and contact your vet as a matter of extreme urgency.

ROAD ACCIDENTS Traffic accidents claim the lives of many cats each year. However, not all accidents prove fatal and it is important that you follow strict rules of first aid in the event of a cat being found by the roadside. It is possible that the cat could be suffering from internal injuries, so try to make a makeshift stretcher (a coat or rug are possibilities), making it as rigid as possible. Slide the cat carefully on to the stretcher, making sure you support the body while avoiding unnecessary movement or jolting the body. Keep the head supported and allow it to lie a little lower than the rest of the body. This will facilitate the blood supply to the brain, reducing the likelihood of brain damage. Keep the cat warm and quiet, and get it to the vet as quickly as possible.

POISONING There are a number of situations in which this can occur and it is often difficult to know exactly what the free-ranging cat may have eaten to make it sick. Cats can be poisoned because they have eaten a rodent, which has itself eaten poison, and **coma**, spontaneous **haemorrhage** and death can be the result. If you suspect this type of poisoning, it is vital to keep the patient warm. Before rushing the cat to the surgery, first telephone the vet who may be able to give important initial advice. Many modern products are safer than their older counterparts, but chemicals commonly used in the house and garden can still be very poisonous to cats; make sure you read labels before using them where animals are about. Medicines intended for humans must in no circumstances be given to cats without advice from your vet. Some medicines, e.g. aspirin, which in the correct dose is safe for humans, may be extremely **toxic** to cats.

Once you are certain that you know what your cat has swallowed, and with veterinary advice, administer an emetic (a strong salt solution), which will make the cat vomit.

In a case of poisoning by a caustic substance, under no circumstances must an emetic be administered as this could cause severe burning to the cat's oesophagus, throat and mouth.

Amanda Edwards, *First Aid for Your Cat*

coma: unconsciousness
haemorrhage: bleeding
toxic: poisonous

Extract 2.3

mizz is a magazine aimed at young teenage girls. Here, the magazine has interviewed a teenager from Tanzania so that young people in the UK can have a glimpse of a different kind of life from theirs.

'I'm Too Poor To Go To School'

We all moan about school, but here's why we shouldn't take it for granted …

FACT FILE:

NAME: Rafra Hasan
AGE: 13
LIVES: Shanty town in Tanzania, East Africa
STAR SIGN: Pisces
LANGUAGE: Swahili
BEST FRIEND: Saida
LOVES: Dancing
HATES: Bullies
SCHOOL: Can't afford to go to school
FAVE BAND: Tanzanian boyband Twingapepeta
FAVE TV PROGRAMME: We don't have electricity, or TVs!
PETS: Used to have a pet cow, but we sold it
MOST RECENT PURCHASE: Food – but I'd love to get some shoes

'My home is a tiny hut in a shanty town on the outskirts of Dar es Salaam, the capital of Tanzania. I live here with my mum. We can't afford shoes so we go barefoot. We sleep on a blanket on the floor and wash in the nearby stream. I hate it here. The whole place smells and is full of rats. But we have nowhere else to go.

Mum and I have been on our own since my dad died two years ago. He was bitten by a mosquito and died of malaria. One week he was okay, the next week he was dead. I miss him so much that I still cry when I think about him.

We used to live in a house at the foot of Mount Kilimanjaro, the tallest mountain in Africa. I loved living there and had my own bedroom. Dad earned money as a farm worker, so I was able to go to school. Because our country is so poor, everyone has to pay to go to school and most people can't afford it, so they miss out. This might sound like fun, but I promise you it isn't. If you don't go to school and learn things, you'll always be poor, so getting an education is your only hope.

I'll bet our school was very different to yours! Our classroom didn't have any doors, or glass in the windows, and the roof was collapsing. Every time it rained we had to go outside under a tree. There were 70 of us in one big class, and we had one textbook between 10 of us. Mum and Dad had to contribute towards everything, even the chalk, so it cost a lot of money.

After Dad died from the mosquito bite, we couldn't afford the rent on our house. Mum decided we should sell our cow and move to Dar es Salaam. Even though it was hard, my family scraped enough money together so I could finish my primary school in the city. You can only go on to secondary school if you pass the exams and I was one of only eight children out of 70 to pass. But because it costs five times more than primary school, there's no way we can afford it.

I'm lucky enough to go to a day centre run by Christian Aid. It's for street kids and for children who are very poor. In the morning we do writing and maths. Most of the kids have never been to school, but I have, so I find the work easy! In the afternoons I learn traditional dancing and acrobatics with my friend Saida.

Right now I spend my days going to the centre, fetching water and firewood for my mother and helping cook whatever food we have. Mum is out trying to find work on market stalls. My dream was to be a maths teacher, but I'll never do that now. Mum thinks my best bet is to be a maid and earn some money.

I really don't want to go away to live with a rich family and do all their cooking and cleaning, but at the moment it's my only option. It's hard for me to imagine what life is like for all the readers of mizz magazine. I want to learn about young people in other countries and I hope by reading my story, you've learned something about life for us in Africa.'

Rafra Hasan, *mizz*, 5th-18th September 2001

Extract 2.4
This passage is from a popular science book in which the aim is to describe how scientists see the world around us in language that everyone can understand. How successful do you think they have been?

Where in the World Are We?

The cosmos
*Our **vantage point** in the universe is a small planet orbiting an average star in a backwater of a large galaxy that is just one of countless others scattered throughout the universe. From our home world – the only place where we know for sure that life exists – we look into space and see the wonders of the cosmos.*

Close to Earth are the planets and other bodies of the solar system orbiting our familiar, life-giving Sun. Farther out are the other stars of our galaxy, some bright and hot, others tiny and dim. We can see gas clouds from which stars spring into existence and detect strange phenomena that show where stars have died in **cataclysmic** violence to leave holes of nothingness behind. There are milky pools that show where other galaxies exist and, stretching the tools of astronomy to their limits, scientists can probe the ultimate mysteries: how the universe could have begun – and how it may meet its end.

vantage point: view point, usually somewhere high up
cataclysmic: enormous, leading to great changes

Our place in space
The movements of the Sun in the sky are governed by the way the Earth moves around the Sun.

The evidence of our eyes suggests that the Sun, because it rises in the east and sets in the west, moves around the Earth. But we have known for a long time that the Earth, our home, is a soccer-ball-shaped planet which turns on its axis once a day and moves around the Sun once a year.

At night, the steady turning of the Earth is evident as the stars, like the Sun and Moon, rise and set. Earth's year-long orbit around the Sun is shown, too, in the way different stars are visible from season to season. It is as if we were on a merry-go-round: our view of the landscape changes as the Earth turns.

But unlike a simple merry-go-round, Earth has an axis which is tilted in relation to the line of its orbit. This means that the Sun is sometimes high in the sky at midday and sometimes low. Our seasons are a constant reminder of this tilt as the Sun travels higher in the sky in summer and lower in winter.

Land, sea and air
The continents are enormous rafts of rock adrift on a molten sea, pushed over the face of the Earth by the slow-moving currents of global convection.

To a visitor from another star system, Earth would stand out among planets orbiting our Sun because from space it looks as if it is almost entirely covered in water. But the oceans are not just low-lying areas that happen to be water-filled. Even if there were no water, there would still be a clear difference between the appearance and activity of the upland areas and the ocean troughs.

At the centres of the ocean areas are vast volcanic ridges, where a type of rock called basalt constantly wells up creating huge 'plates' of material. Driven by the convection currents of material rising from the Earth's molten interior, the rock slowly moves outward from these mid-ocean ridges, causing sea-floor spreading and pushing the plates along. The plates move over the underlying material at the rate of a few centimetres a year.

Earth's continents are giant rafts up to 160 km (100 miles) thick sitting on top of the plates. Some 200 million years ago, there was just one landmass but this broke up to form today's continents. Where plates have collided vast mountain ranges such as the Himalayas and the Alps have arisen; where they slip past each other a series of earthquakes occurs; where one plate disappears beneath another deep ocean trenches form and volcanic action takes place.

Gases belched out during volcanic eruptions over millions of years gave Earth its initial atmosphere, which was changed by geological action and by plants converting carbon dioxide to oxygen. The make-up of air has settled at 77 per cent nitrogen, 21 per cent oxygen, 1 per cent water vapour and smaller amounts of argon, carbon dioxide, neon, helium and sulphur. Earth's gravitational field is strong enough to stop the atmosphere leaking away into space.

Origins of life

*The rich diversity of life on Earth became possible when chance threw together a combination of chemicals in **a structure that could copy itself**.*

Our world seethes with life. Living things are found almost everywhere on our planet's surface, from the lush forests of the tropics to the extraordinary 'dry valleys' of Antarctica, where hardly any moisture has fallen in thousands of years. The cleanest operating theatre contains microscopic bacteria, and ordinary houses shelter millions of living things, from tiny fungi to mites and insects. But how did all this life first appear?

For many people, the existence of life on Earth can be explained only by a special act of creation. But evidence from fossils suggests that life has existed on Earth for billions of years and has gradually changed and developed as time has gone by. When the Earth was young – over four billion years ago – it was too hot to support life and its surface was bombarded by meteors hurtling in from space. Gradually Earth cooled and developed a skin of water. It is in this global ocean that life probably began.

The ancient ocean was a huge vat of simple chemical compounds. The atoms that made up these compounds constantly changed partners. Sometimes atoms joined to form bigger, more complex compounds. But sooner or later, these broke up, and vanished without trace.

---

a structure that could copy itself: see the last paragraph of the passage

Life became possible only when an extraordinary chance threw together a compound that could make copies of itself. Like a chain of magnets, it attracted its own chemical components, lining them up to form a new chain. Then the new chain broke free and, in turn, made copies of itself. Life had begun.

Science Explained, **ed. Colin A. Ronan**

Extract 2.5

In this article from the *BBC History* magazine, Deborah Partridge describes an event that happened in the last century, in which the children of a small village in Norfolk went on strike in support of their teachers.

When the Kids Were United

One of the longest strikes in British history took place not in a hotbed of urban class struggle, but in a tiny village school in the rural backwaters of Norfolk

This month sees a rally to mark one of the longest and most remarkable strikes in British history, a dispute which holds unique significance for the Labour movement. It is unusual because it started, not in some grimy factory, but in a tiny village school in one of the quietest corners of Norfolk. It is also extraordinary because it lasted for 25 years, beginning in 1914 and ending with the death of the husband of the school's headmistress on the eve of the Second World War.

The beginning of the strike at Burston school, near Diss, coincided with the appointment of new teaching staff, who arrived to find the classroom in a **dilapidated** state – and empty of pupils. The children were outside the school gates, demonstrating

---

dilapidated: run down

with placards, screaming for 'justice', and demanding the return of their old teachers.

But what were they protesting about? Twelve years before, Balfour's Education Act had encouraged the new local education authorities to open grammar schools in every town – and **inadvertently** condemned country children to second-rate schooling, as better pay and resources drew the best teachers into towns. For those left out in the cold, school was a grim experience. Many rural schools were falling down, with classrooms damp, badly maintained and barely heated. Sons and daughters of agricultural labourers were often removed from lessons when farmers needed them to pick crops.

It was in this environment that the children of Burston on the Norfolk/Suffolk border grew up. Most of them were pitifully poor – their fathers worked on the windswept **arable land** that surrounds the village, earning no more than £35 a year. But, from 1911, the youngsters were lucky in having two of the most visionary and dedicated teachers in the country.

Tom and Kitty Higdon challenged the educational *status quo* at every level. Both

---

inadvertently: unintentionally, without meaning to
arable land: land suitable for growing crops on

were Christian Socialists who practised **child-centred** teaching long before it was established policy. They made formal complaints about the condition of the school and encouraged their pupils to think of themselves as more than labourers or domestic servants and to form their own opinions. Kitty even took her own typewriter into school and taught the girls to type in her spare time, and her husband came into conflict with the local tenant farmers whenever he complained about pupils working in the fields.

The children responded to this inspirational couple with enthusiasm and affection. So, when the Higdons were sacked by the school's managing body (a conflict sparked in part when, without the

child-centred: giving priority to the needs of children

permission of the school managers, Kitty lit the school fire one wet morning to dry the pupils' soaked clothes), the children took the law into their own hands. Their organiser was 13-year-old Violet Potter.

'Just before this, there had been a whole series of children's strikes across Britain,' says Tony Jeffs, a lecturer in community education at Durham University. 'It was a period of dock strikes and widespread industrial unrest. Children had picked up on this and had walked out of about 50 schools.

'What made this different and genuinely set it apart was that Burston was not about teacher cruelty or bad treatment. It was the reverse – the kids had seen a better way of education and they didn't want to lose it.' He has no doubt that Violet Potter was the ringleader, though she had the backing of most of the pupils' parents. Violet collected the names of children willing to take action on the afternoon of 31 March 1914, the day before the strike began. Sixty-six out of the 72 children on the register were ready to take a stand. The following morning, as the Higdons handed over the keys to their successors, the children marched through the village to the sound of Violet's concertina, waving banners saying: "We want our teachers back."

The children's route took them right round the village, singing and shouting their demands. One of their main targets was the rector, the Reverend Charles Tucker Eland, a school manager who had objected to the fire-lighting incident and what he perceived as a lack of courtesy from Kitty (who, on one occasion, had refused to curtsy to his family).

The Reverend Eland takes his revenge

The Rev Eland took his revenge by persuading two **Barnardo's** girls, who were being cared for in the village, to falsely claim that Kitty Higdon had beaten them and it was this that precipitated the teachers' sacking.

'The parson got two Barnardo children to say that our governess had caned them and slapped their faces,' Emily Wilby observed coolly, 'but we all knew she did not.' The Higdons demanded an inquiry, and involved the National Union of Teachers, but to no avail. Despite the caning charge not being proved, they were told to go.

The rector had achieved his purpose and, when he saw the resulting parade around the village green, he dismissed it as an April Fool's joke. Little did he realise that

Barnardo's: a home for destitute children

he was witnessing the beginning of one of the longest protests ever recorded.

The pupils marched again on several occasions, and, with the strike attracting attention from the school authorities, parents were soon summoned to court in Diss for failing to send their children to school. They were summoned back to court several times before a decision was made to teach the striking children on the village green. Every morning the youngsters would gather on the grass and Kitty would hold an outdoor registration, before proceeding with classes more or less as normal. The county's education committee were horrified and sent their attendance officer to Burston, where he stood on the edge of the green conspicuously making notes. He then visited the pupils' homes and **harangued** their parents – but they were determined not to be intimidated and refused to send their children back to the county school. Only six or seven children were still being taught there by the new teachers.

A local strike goes national

Fortunately for the first few weeks of this unconventional arrangement the weather

---

harangued: made speeches to, nagged, shouted at

was good. When it turned wet, an empty cottage and, later, a redundant carpenter's shop were offered to the strikers. 'Sam Sandy came and whitewashed it out and mended the windows,' records Emily Wilby. 'He put a ladder up so we could go upstairs.'

Meanwhile, newspaper reports of what was going on in this remote part of East Anglia were reaching London. Leading figures in the Labour movement and the women's suffrage campaign took up the cause.

Despite the swell of support, there's no doubt the strikers' families suffered real hardship. Many agricultural labourers rented **glebe land** from the Church where they grew vegetables and kept chickens. As the conflict in the village deepened, the Rev Eland threw them off the meadow and destroyed their crops.

But despite intimidation from the rector, the parents 'stuck like glue', to use local fish-seller George Durbridge's phrase. After many months of struggle, donations started pouring in from cooperative societies and unions such as the National Union of Railwaymen, bringing in enough money to build a permanent 'strike school'. The

---

glebe land: land suitable for growing vegetables, belonging to the parson

simple, single-storey building, very similar
to a Methodist chapel, was constructed in
the heart of Burston beside the village
green. It was ready to open in 1917.

'Forever a school of freedom'

The honours were done by a triumphant
Violet, by now aged 17. On the morning of
May 13, at a ceremony attended by many of
those who had given money, she led the
pupils into what was one of the most
modern and well-equipped primary schools
in East Anglia, saying: 'With joy and
thankfulness, I declare this school open, to
be forever a school of freedom.' Kitty was
applauded on her way in.

Within a few years the Rev Eland left the
village, and the strike school, which
completely overshadowed the almost
empty council school less than a quarter of
a mile away, was being seen as a model
educational establishment.

Today, the strike school is still standing,
though it is now a museum and monument
to Burston's **unassailable** place in Labour
history.

Deborah Partridge, *BBC History,* September 2001

unassailable: untouchable, unquestionable

Extract 2.6

This article is taken from a magazine for women who are about to have or have just had a baby. The article aims to inform new mothers about what babies are like and how to care for them. As you read it, you might like to think about how successful the writer has been in her aim of providing information and reassurance for new mothers. In particular, what is the writer's tone of voice, and how does she convey it?

The Truth About New Babies

After months of preparation, your baby is finally here. But in the first few weeks things aren't quite as you expected.

As a new parent, your newborn baby is the most fascinating little creature in the world, but she's also a bit of a mystery. Her skin may be spotty or wrinkly, she'll make funny noises and her eyes will follow you. You'll spend hours watching her, amazed and delighted by each new thing you discover. Here we help you to understand why new babies do what they do.

♨ SHE KNOWS HER MUM

It used to be thought that babies couldn't recognise faces until they were several months old, but according to Lynne Murray, Professor of Developmental Psychology at the University of Reading, they know their mum from the start. 'We now know that babies can hear while they're still in the womb,' explains Professor Murray, 'so as soon as they're born, they'll recognise their mother's voice. They can also taste

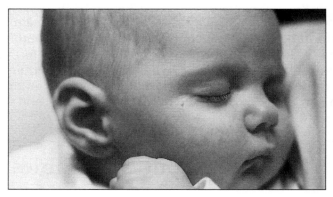

while still in the womb, and the taste of amniotic fluid
is related to the smell and taste of breastmilk. In a way,
then, a baby is geared to anticipate her mother's voice
and smell even before birth.' Within a few hours of
birth, a newborn will watch her mother's face intently
and, if taken from her, will turn her head towards her
voice. Within two or three days, your baby will know
your face from others.

Top tip 'Your baby is able to see eight to 12 inches
clearly from birth – exactly the distance you'll
naturally position your face when you're talking to
and playing with her,' says Professor Murray.

 SHE LOVES A CUDDLE
Touch is a very important part of the bonding process.
Your newborn has been safe inside you for nine
months and is now out in the big wide world on her
own, so feeling your arms around her will help her to
feel snug and secure. She'll love the close contact as

she's being fed, the touch of your skin soothing her.

'The amount of time you spend holding your baby will depend largely on your lifestyle and other commitments,' says Professor Murray. 'But most babies love to be held and there's no way you can 'spoil' them by cuddling them too much.'

Top tip Holding her close to your chest will enable her to hear your heartbeat and smell your milk, both of which will help soothe and reassure her.

✿ SHE DECIDES HOW MUCH TO EAT AND WHEN

When breastfeeding, your baby may seem hungry all the time. As breastmilk is digested so quickly and easily, it won't stay in the stomach for long. 'A newborn's stomach is only about the size of a walnut,' says Margaret Lawson, senior lecturer in paediatric nutrition at the Institute of Child Health. 'It's not designed to take large feeds.' If your newborn is very sleepy, talk to your midwife about how long you can leave her between feeds, but generally she should want to eat at least every four hours.

'Most babies are born with an efficient appetite – they'll fall asleep when they're full and wake when they're empty,' says Margaret Lawson. 'It's possible to overfeed on formula milk, usually because the mum worries her baby isn't taking the amount she's 'supposed' to and persuades her to take more. Little and often is best in the first couple of weeks.'

Top tip Breast or bottle, try to feed on demand.

🐣 SHE KNOWS YOUR VOICE

Ever noticed how adults adjust the way they speak when talking to babies? Nature has programmed us to do this. 'We don't know why,' says Professor Murray, 'but babies respond to the way we automatically change the pitch, speed and intonation of our speech when we talk to them. We do this **intuitively** in every culture across the world, despite a huge variety of languages. It's a natural instinct.'

Top tip Talk about anything and everything – it's the tone, not the words she'll hear.

🐣 HER WEIGHT WILL DROP AT FIRST

Your baby will lose between five and ten per cent of her weight in her first week. This can be worrying for a new mum, but it's perfectly normal. 'Most of the weight lost is due to the loss of fluid and meconium (a baby's first bowel movements),' says Margaret Lawson. 'Babies may lose a tiny amount of fat, but they're born with a store of fat, so they're designed to cope with this. Most babies will be back up to their birthweight after ten days and may even have gained some extra weight.'

Top tip This is normal, so try not to worry.

🐣 SHE CAN CRY AND CRY – AND CRY

It can be distressing when your new baby seems to cry relentlessly, but bear in mind it's the only way she can

---

intuitively: instinctively

attract your attention. Before long, you'll get used to her cries and what they mean. She may be telling you that her nappy needs changing, that she's hungry, has wind, or is too hot or cold. If you've fed, changed and winded her but she cries as soon as you put her down, it could be that she's bored or lonely, or that she wants the security and comfort of being held. 'Some babies are just shocked to find themselves here,' says Margaret Lawson. 'They've been snug inside the womb for nine months and the change of environment can be unsettling at first.'

Top tip The sound of your voice may soothe her, so singing or talking softly may help. Alternatively, you could try rocking her, walking around with her in a sling, **swaddling** her or even taking her out for a drive in the car.

☽ SHE DOESN'T KNOW YOU SLEEP AT NIGHT

While newborns can sleep for around 16 out of every 24 hours, the books don't tell you that those hours may not all be at night – and they certainly won't be in one chunk. Babies have no concept of the difference between night and day and they may wake every hour throughout the night. The first few weeks tend to be the most difficult and at around six weeks, she'll start to establish her own sleep pattern.

You may find it helpful to introduce a bedtime routine as a way of teaching her when it's time to

---

swaddling: wrapping in cloths or blankets

sleep – perhaps a bath, then a feed, then a story followed by a kiss and a cuddle before she snuggles down for the night. Broken nights can be difficult to deal with, especially when you're already exhausted with caring for your new baby. But remember this phase won't last forever – you will get through it.

🐣 JUST TOPPING AND TAILING IS FINE

It's best not to bath her daily, at least until the bellybutton has completely healed. The umbilical cord shrivels up within a few days and the stump will drop off after about a fortnight. Try to keep the area around the cord dry until this happens and let the air get to it when you can. For the first few weeks, topping and tailing is all she should need. Clean her bottom with warm water and cotton wool, or a mild baby lotion.

Top tip Avoid using wipes regularly as they may contain alcohol, perfumes or other ingredients that could irritate her skin.

🐣 SHE MAKES A LOT OF NOISES

You may be surprised when your baby starts sneezing and hiccupping, snorting and rattling. Any sneezing is probably down to the fact that her tiny nasal passages haven't yet grown the little hairs needed to filter out dust particles and hiccups may be caused by air swallowed during a feed.

Top tip Just remember, the noises are normal, and part of her initial growth and development.

Susan Elliot-Wright, *Prima Baby*, October 2001

Extract 2.7
Orienteering is a sport that is increasing in strength and becoming more and more popular in schools. In this extract from a book about orienteering and the skills needed to do well in it, Carol McNeill describes the background to the sport and how it is played.

Orienteering

Orienteering is a running sport. The competitive orienteer runs with a map and compass, choosing his own way, to find a fixed number of control points which are marked very precisely on the map, and are indicated in the terrain by a large red and white control marker. At each control point a 'pin punch' is attached for each competitor to mark his or her control card and therefore prove that the control has been visited. A code number or letters, also fixed to the control, establishes that it is the correct control on the course. The course will vary between one and thirteen kilometres, with six to thirty control points. The distance and technical difficulty will depend on age, sex, experience and fitness. Within each class, it is the person finding all the controls in the right order in the shortest time who wins.

History
Orienteering was introduced to Britain in the early 1960s having already become well established as a sport in the Scandinavian countries. The Swedes were the **pioneers**. One of the first official events was organised

---

pioneers: forerunners, the first to do it

by Major Ernst Killander in 1918 as a result of his concern for a falling interest in athletics and a lack of use of the forest environment. It has grown since then to become one of the most popular sports in Sweden.

It was a Swede, Baron 'Rak' Lagerfelt who had a major influence in establishing the sport in Britain. South Ribble Orienteering Club, Southern Navigators, and Edinburgh Southern Orienteering Club were the first of over 150 different clubs which now cover the whole of the United Kingdom . . .

The growth of the sport has been largely influenced by the improvement in the quality of maps. The early events were dependent on copies of the **Ordnance Survey maps**. Now, with advances in printing technology, most events are able to provide a specially drawn large-scale map in five colours for each competitor. The areas are surveyed and the map drawn by orienteers using internationally recognised drawing specifications. 5 metre or 2.5 metre contours show the precise shape of the terrain and other details such as large boulders, pits, gullies, depressions and small crags which enable the orienteer to know exactly where he is all the time, as well as providing a large number of potential control sites.

A sport for all

At its most competitive the sport offers a lot to the athlete who likes to think, as well as run. The sport is also organised to offer a challenge to children and adults of all ages and athletic ability. String courses for the

---

Ordnance Survey maps: official maps of the British Isles, originally drawn up for the army under the supervision of the Master-General of the Ordnance ('ordnance' means heavy artillery)

under-tens allow even three or four-year-old children to enjoy running through woodland and finding controls, whilst classes for the veterans, in five year age groupings from thirty-five to seventy, give an opportunity for athletes and non-athletes alike to participate in a running sport at whatever level they choose. Walking round a course with accurate map reading may not put you at the top of your class but it will certainly not put you at the bottom. **The story of the tortoise and the hare** can be aptly applied to this sport.

Orienteering gives you confidence in handling a map and compass in any navigation situation, whether it is negotiating your local footpaths or exploring wilderness areas on the other side of the world. It will take you into some of our most attractive woodland, forest, heath and moorland, many of which are not normally accessible to the public. In being privileged to go into these areas you should also develop an appreciation for its conservation . . .

Orienteering is the most enjoyable and fulfilling sport I know. Running fast and effortlessly through mature woodland is an aesthetic experience and finding control points never ceases to keep its magic.

Carol McNeill, *Orienteering: The Skills of the Game*

the story of the tortoise and the hare: one of the stories told in Aesop's Fables; Aesop was a sixth-century Greek story-teller, who told the tale of a hare who was so sure of being able to outrun a tortoise that, during a race with the tortoise, he flitted about, got distracted, took a break, while all the time the tortoise plodded steadily on and reached the finishing line first.

Extract 2.8

This passage comes from a book published in the 1950s. In it Rehna Cloete describes her life as a young American woman in Paris, and how she met and 'caught' the man who later became her husband. Here she talks about ways for a woman to behave to make herself attractive to a man.

The Philosophy of Catching Your Man

Philosophy is very important to a girl, being the key to life and its explanation. Though of course a girl should not go too deeply into it, and the philosophy of small brown-haired girls is quite different from that of big brunettes. We see different worlds, even height makes a difference. For instance, I thought, it must be wonderful to see the tops of people's heads all the time which I only do if they are sitting down. But men were the most interesting to study. It is very hard to please most men, because they want a friend, a wife, a mistress, a good cook, someone who dresses well but cheaply, and is so attractive that people say how nice she looks, but not attractive enough to make them turn around or follow her on the street. She must be smart enough to understand what he says, but a good listener too. She must also like what he likes – the ballet, or ball games, horses, deep-sea fishing, golf, tennis, chess or bridge. She

---

philosophy: originally, in Ancient Greek, this meant the love of wisdom (*philo* comes from the Greek verb 'to love', and *Sophia* was the goddess of wisdom); now it more usually describes the study of things, what they are and how they came to be so

must like the same film stars, and this is where philosophy comes in, because if she is philosophical she can take all these things in her stride. There remains what is called sex, which is no problem because it comes naturally to a girl, all she has to do is be there, as it were, the right girl (or even the wrong girl) in the right place at the right time.

Rebounds are very good things because then even the wrong girl may get her man. It's like having coffee ice cream when there is no chocolate, if he is in an ice cream mood, because then almost anyone will do.

On the other hand, men are much nicer than girls because they have more sense and you can guess what they will do next. Even I can do that. What I have never figured out is what they will do after that.

When you have classified your memories you can have better guesses. They come under headings as stamps do for countries. There are techniques for a **picture house**, a church picnic, a beach, moonlight anywhere, on shipboard, in a car, and so on. The better collection of memories a girl has, the better she is equipped in a philosophical sort of way to meet each new emergency, and some are really good too, as I've found out. What a man does depends on where he is, and what he has had to eat and drink. Sometimes it's just right, sometimes he just goes to sleep, or else tries to do too much.

Rehna 'Tiny' Cloete, *To Catch a Man?*

---

rebounds: when people 'bounce back' from broken relationships
picture house: cinema

Extract 2.9

In this passage from his autobiography, Oskar Kokoschka describes his feelings as he is shot by Russian soldiers during the First World War.

With Austrian Cavalry on the Eastern Front

August 1915

There was something stirring at the edge of the forest. Dismount! Lead horses! Our line was joined by volunteers, and **we beat forward into the bushes as if we were going to shoot pheasant.** The enemy was withdrawing deeper into the forest, firing only **sporadically**. So we had to mount again, which was always the worst part, for since **conscription** had been introduced the **requisitioned** horses were as gun-shy as the reservists who had been called up were wretched horsemen. After all, most of them were used to sitting only on an office chair. In the forest suddenly we were met by a hail of bullets so near and so thick

---

we beat forward into the bushes as if we were going to shoot pheasant: on a pheasant shoot, beaters go before the hunting party, beating the bushes with sticks in order to make the pheasant fly up so they can be shot

sporadically: once in a while, every so often

conscription: compulsory military service (as opposed to volunteers and professional soldiers)

requisitioned: taken for use by the army

that one seemed to see each bullet flitting past; it was like a startled swarm of wasps. Charge! Now the great day had come, the day for which I too had been longing. I still had enough presence of mind to urge my mount forward and to one side, out of the throng of other horses that had now gone wild, as if chased by ghosts, the congestion being made worse by more coming up from the rear and galloping over fallen men and beasts. I wanted to settle this thing on my own and to look the enemy straight in the face. A hero's death – fair enough! But I had no wish to be trampled to death like a worm. The Russians had lured us into a trap. I had actually set eyes on the Russian machine-gun before I felt a dull blow on my temple.

The sun and the moon were both shining at once and my head ached like mad. What on earth was I to do with this scent of flowers? Some flower – I couldn't remember its name however I racked my brains. And all that yelling round me and the moaning of the wounded, which seemed to fill the whole forest – that must have been what brought me round. Good lord, they must be in agony! Then I became absorbed by the fact that I couldn't control the cavalry boot with the leg in it, which was moving about too far away, although it belonged to me. I recognized the boot by the spur: contrary to regulations, my spurs had no sharp **rowels**. Over on the grass there were two captains in Russian uniform dancing a ballet, running up and kissing each other on the cheeks

rowel: a rotating star or disk at the end of a spur, often with very sharp points

like two young girls. That would have been against regulations in our army. I had a tiny round hole in my head. My horse, lying on top of me, had lashed out one last time before dying, and that had brought me to my senses. I tried to say something, but my mouth was stiff with blood, which was beginning to congeal. The shadows all round me were growing huger and huger, and I wanted to ask how it was that the sun and the moon were both shining at the same time. I wanted to point at the sky, but my arm wouldn't move. Perhaps I lay there unconscious for several days.

Oskar Kokoschka, *The Faber Book of Reportage,* ed. John Carey

Extract 2.10
Bill Bryson is an American author who writes popular and amusing books about the different places he has visited around the world. In this passage he describes a trip to Liverpool.

Soaking in Port Sunlight

I took a train to Liverpool. They were having a festival of litter when I arrived. Citizens had taken time off from their busy activities to add crisp packets, empty cigarette boxes, and carrier-bags to the otherwise bland and neglected landscape. They fluttered gaily in the bushes and brought colour and texture to pavements and gutters. And to think that elsewhere we stick these objects in rubbish bags.

In another bout of extravagant madness, I had booked a room in the Adelphi Hotel. I had seen it from the street on earlier visits and it appeared to have an old-fashioned grandeur about it that I was keen to investigate. On the other hand, it looked expensive and I wasn't sure my trousers could stand another session in the trouser press. So I was most agreeably surprised when I checked in to discover that I was entitled to a special weekend rate and that there would be money to spare for a nice meal and a parade of beer in any of the many wonderful pubs in which Liverpool specialises . . .

Here's a piece of advice for you. Don't go on the Mersey ferry unless you are prepared to have the famous song by Gerry and the Pacemakers running through your head for about eleven days afterwards. They play it when you board the ferry and they play it when you get off and for quite a lot of time in between. I went on it the following morning thinking a bit of a sitdown and a cruise on the water would be just the way to ease myself out of a killer hangover, but in fact the inescapable sound of 'Ferry 'cross the Mersey' only worsened my cranial plight. Apart from that, it must be said that the Mersey ferry is an agreeable, if decidedly breezy, way of passing a morning. It's a bit like the Sydney Harbour cruise, but without Sydney.

When they weren't playing 'Ferry 'cross the Mersey', they played a soundtrack outlining the famous sights from the deck, but the acoustics were terrible and 80 per cent of whatever was said was instantly blown away on the wind. All I could hear were snatches of things like '3 million' and 'world's biggest' but whether they were talking about oil refinery capacity or **Derek Hatton**'s suits I couldn't say. But the gist of it was that *this* was once a great city and now it's Liverpool.

Now don't get me wrong. I'm exceedingly fond of Liverpool. It's probably my favourite English city. But it does rather feel like a place with more past than future. Leaning on a deck rail gazing out on miles of motionless waterfront, it was impossible to believe that until quite recently – and for two hundred proud and prosperous years before that – Liverpool's 10 miles of docks and shipyards provided employment for 100,000 people, directly or indirectly. Tobacco from Africa and Virginia, palm oil from the South Pacific, copper from Chile, **jute** from India, and almost any other commodity you could care to name passed through here on its way to being made into something useful. So too, no less significantly, did some ten million people bound for a new life in the

---

Derek Hatton: a Liverpool politician of the 1970s, famous for his elegant suits

jute: a plant fibre, which used to be imported from India for making canvas, ropes and so on

new world, drawn by stories of streets paved with gold and the possibility of accumulating immense personal wealth, or in the case of my own forebears by the giddy prospect of spending the next century and a half dodging tornadoes and shovelling snow in Iowa.

Liverpool became the third richest city in the empire. Only London and Glasgow had more millionaires. By 1880 it was generating more tax revenue than Birmingham, Bristol, Leeds and Sheffield together even though collectively they had twice the population. Cunard and White Star Lines had their headquarters in Liverpool, and there were countless other lines, now mostly forgotten – Blue Funnel, Bank Line, Coast Line, Pacific Steam Line, McAndrews Lines, Elder Dempster, Booth. There were more lines operating out of Liverpool then than there are ships today, or so at least it can seem when there is nothing much along the waterfront but the ghostly warble of Gerry Marsden's voice.

The decline happened in a single generation. In 1966, Liverpool was still the second busiest port in Britain, after London. By 1985, it had fallen so low that it was smaller and quieter than even Tees and Hartlepool, Grimsby and Immingham. But in its heyday it was something special. Maritime commerce brought Liverpool not just wealth and employment, but an air of cosmopolitanism that few cities in the world could rival, and it still has that sense about it. In Liverpool, you still feel like you are some place.

I walked from the ferry to the Albert Dock. There were plans at one time to drain it and turn it into a car park – it seems a miracle sometimes that there is anything at all left in this poor, stumbling country – but now, of course, they have been scrubbed up and gentrified, the old warehouses turned into offices, flats and restaurants for the sort of people who carry telephones in their briefcases. It also incorporates an outpost of the Tate Gallery and the Merseyside Maritime Museum.

I love the Merseyside Maritime Museum, not merely because it is well done but because it gives such a potent sense of what Liverpool was like when it was a great port – indeed when the world was full of a productive busyness and majesty of enterprise that it seems utterly to have lost now. How I'd love to have lived in an age when one could walk to a waterfront and see mighty ships unloading great squares of cotton fibre and heavy brown bags of coffee and spices, and when every sailing involved hundreds of people – sailors and dockers and throngs of excited passengers. Today, you go to a waterfront and all you find is an endless expanse of battered containers and one guy in an elevated cabin shunting them about.

Once there was infinite romance in the sea, and the Merseyside Maritime Museum captures every bit of it. I was particularly taken with an upstairs room full of outsized ships' models – the sort that must have once decorated executive boardrooms. Gosh, they were wonderful. Even as models they were wonderful. All the great Liverpool ships were here – the *Titanic*, the *Imperator*, the RMS *Majestic* (which began life as the *Bismarck* and was seized as **war reparations**) and the unutterably lovely TSS *Vauban* with its broad decks of polished maple and its jaunty funnels. According to its label, it was owned by the Liverpool, Brazil and River Plate Steam Navigation Company Limited. Just reading those words, I was seized with a dull ache at the thought that never again will we see such a beautiful thing. J.B. Priestley called them the greatest constructions of the modern world, our equivalent of cathedrals, and he was absolutely right. I was appalled to think that never in my life would I have an opportunity to stride down a gangplank in a panama hat and a white suit and go looking for a bar with

---

war reparations: fines imposed on Germany after the First World War

a revolving ceiling fan. How crushingly unfair life can sometimes be.

I spent two hours wandering through the museum, looking with care at all the displays. I would happily have stayed longer, but I had to check out of the hotel, so I regretfully departed and walked back through central Liverpool's fine Victorian streets to the Adelphi, where I grabbed my things and checked out.

I had a slight hankering to go to Port Sunlight, the model community built in 1888 by William Lever to house his soap workers, as I was interested to see how it compared with Saltaire. So I went to Liverpool Central and caught a train. At Rock Ferry we were informed that because of engineering works we would have to complete the journey by bus. This was OK by me because I was in no hurry and you can always see more from a bus. We rode along the Wirral Peninsula for some time before the driver announced the stop for Port Sunlight. I was the only person to get off, and the most striking thing about it was that this was patently not Port Sunlight. I tapped on the front doors and waited for them to gasp open.

'Excuse me,' I said, 'but this doesn't look like Port Sunlight.'

'That's because it's Bebington,' he said. 'It's as close as I can get to Port Sunlight because of a low bridge.'

Oh.

'So where exactly is Port Sunlight then?' I asked but it was to a cloud of blue smoke. I hooked my rucksack over a shoulder and set off along a road that I hoped might be the right one – and no doubt would have been had I taken another. I walked for some distance, but the road seemed to go nowhere, or at least nowhere that looked Port Sunlightish . . .

I returned to Bebington where I sought directions in a shop, which I should have done in the first place, of course. Port Sunlight, it turned out, was just down the road, under a railway bridge and over a junction – or perhaps it was the other way round. I don't know because it was now pouring with rain and I tucked my head so low into my shoulders that I didn't see much of anything.

I walked for perhaps half a mile, but it was worth every sodden step. Port Sunlight was lovely, a proper little garden community, and much cheerier in aspect than the huddled stone cottages of Saltaire. This had open green spaces and a pub and pretty little houses half hidden behind drifts of foliage. There wasn't a soul about and nothing seemed to be open – neither the shops nor the pub nor the heritage centre nor the Lady Lever Art Gallery, all of which was a bit of a downer – but I made the best of things by having a slog round the rainy streets. I was a bit surprised to see a factory still there, still churning out soap as far as I could tell, and then I realized that I had exhausted all that Port Sunlight had to offer on a rainy Saturday out of season. So I trudged back to the bus-stop where I had so recently alighted and waited an hour and a quarter in a driving rain for a bus onward to Hooton, which was even less fun than it sounds.

Bill Bryson, *Notes From a Small Island*

Extract 2.11

On 6 August 1945, towards the end of the Second World War, the Americans dropped the world's first atomic bomb on the Japanese city of Hiroshima. Marcel Junod was one of the first journalists taken to see the ruins of the city at the end of the war.

Visiting Hiroshima

9 September 1945

The bare cone of Fujiyama was just visible on the horizon as we flew over the 'inland sea' which lay beneath us like a lavender-blue carpet picked out in green and yellow with its numerous promontories and wooded islands ...

Towards midday a huge white patch appeared on the ground below us. This chalky desert, looking almost like ivory in the sun, surrounded by a crumble of twisted ironwork and ash heaps, was all that remained of Hiroshima ...

The journalist described the main official buildings of the town, which were built of reinforced concrete and dominated a sea of low-roofed Japanese houses extending over six miles to the wooded hills I could see in the distance.

'On August 6th there wasn't a cloud in the sky above Hiroshima, and a mild, hardly perceptible wind blew from the south. Visibility was almost perfect for ten or twelve miles.

'At nine minutes past seven in the morning an air-raid warning sounded and four American B-29 planes appeared. At 7.31 the all clear was given. Feeling themselves in safety people came out of their shelters and went about their affairs and the work of the day began.

'Suddenly a glaring whitish pinkish light appeared in the sky accompanied by an unnatural tremor which was followed almost immediately by a wave of suffocating heat and a wind which swept away everything in its path.

'Within a few seconds the thousands of people in the streets and the gardens in the centre of the town were scorched by a wave of searing heat. Many were killed instantly, others lay writhing on the ground screaming in agony from the intolerable pain of their burns. Everything standing upright in the way of the blast, walls, houses, factories and other buildings, was **annihilated** and the debris spun round in a whirlwind and was carried up into the air. Trains were flung off the rails as if they were toys. Horses, dogs and cattle suffered the same fate as human beings. Every living thing was petrified in an attitude of indescribable suffering. Even the vegetation did not escape. Trees went up in flames, the rice plants lost their greenness, the grass burned on the ground like dry straw.

'Beyond the zone of utter death in which nothing remained alive houses collapsed in a whirl of beams, bricks and girders. Up to about three miles from the centre of the explosion lightly built houses were flattened as though they had been built of cardboard. Those who were inside were either killed or wounded. Those who managed to extricate themselves by some miracle found themselves surrounded by a ring of fire. And the few who succeeded in making their way to safety generally died twenty to thirty days later from the delayed effects of the deadly gamma rays. Some of the reinforced concrete or stone buildings remained standing but their interiors were completely gutted by the blast.

'About half an hour after the explosion whilst the sky all around Hiroshima was still cloudless a fine rain began to fall on the town and went on for about five minutes. It was caused by the sudden rise of over-heated air to a great height, where it condensed and fell back as rain. Then a violent wind rose and the fires extended with terrible rapidity, because most Japanese houses are built only of timber and straw.

---

annihilated: wiped out, utterly destroyed

'By the evening the fire began to die down and then it went out. There was nothing left to burn. Hiroshima had ceased to exist.'

The Japanese broke off and then pronounced one word with indescribable but restrained emotion: 'Look.'

We were then rather less than four miles away from the Aioi Bridge, which was immediately beneath the explosion, but already the roofs of the houses around us had lost their tiles and the grass was yellow along the roadside. At three miles from the centre of the devastation the houses were already destroyed, their roofs had fallen in and the beams jutted out from the wreckage of their walls. But so far it was only the usual spectacle presented by towns damaged by ordinary high explosives.

About two and a half miles from the centre of the town all the buildings had been burnt out and destroyed. Only traces of the foundations and piles of debris and rusty charred ironwork were left. This zone was like the devastated areas of Tokyo, Osaka and Kobé after the mass fall of incendiaries.

At three-quarters of a mile from the centre of the explosion nothing at all was left. Everything had disappeared. It was a stony waste littered with debris and twisted girders. The incandescent breath of the fire had swept away every obstacle and all that remained upright were one or two fragments of stone walls and a few stoves which had remained incongruously on their base.

We got out of the car and made our way slowly through the ruins into the centre of the dead city. Absolute silence reigned in the whole **necropolis**.

Marcel Junod, *The Faber Book of Reportage*, ed. John Carey

---

necropolis: city of the dead, cemetery (from the Ancient Greek *necros* meaning 'corpse' and *polis* meaning 'city')

Extract 2.12

This article comes from *Focus*, a popular science magazine. Here the magazine examines the issue of air pollution in Great Britain. As you read, see if you can decide on the point of view taken in the article. Is it as detached as it appears?

Every Breath You Take

The statistics on air quality are contradictory – what are we to believe?

SHOCKING FACT NO 1: Last year in London more people died from illnesses related to traffic pollution than were killed in road accidents

A report looking at the links between health and transport in the capital has calculated that around 380 people died from causes related to pollution last year, compared with 226 fatalities from road accidents. Transport emissions are also reducing life expectancy, knocking about 34,000 years off London residents' lives every year. More uncertain statistically, but even more worrying, is the estimated half a million people who suffer from minor respiratory complaints as a result of transport-related pollution.

A spokesman for the campaign group Transport 2000 is not surprised by these numbers. 'Nationally, it is estimated that 24,000 people die prematurely from pollution-related illnesses, while just 3,400 are killed on the roads,' he says. However, Joe Buchdahl, information officer at the Atmosphere, Climate and Environment Information Programme (ACE) at Manchester Metropolitan University, says the ill-health figures rather than the fatalities are what we should worry about. 'Of course a person can have a fatal asthma attack triggered by diesel fumes but, in the main, pollution exacerbates poor health,' he says.

So how many people are dangerously **susceptible to** poor air quality? Tim Brown, policy director at the National Society for Clean Air (NSCA), says there's no definite answer but, at a conference earlier this year, scientists began to guesstimate the

---

susceptible to: affected by

numbers. 'There is probably a small number of people on the point of death that are tipped over the edge by pollution,' he says. 'Then there are maybe five per cent of the population who are frail and susceptible that have to go to hospital or become ill as a result of pollution. Pollution could bring their death forward, in some instances, by years. Certainly, deaths and hospital admissions increase within a couple of days of a bad smog episode. There is a very strong correlation.'

SHOCKING FACT NO 2: The urban air quality figures for 2000 are the best on record

Although it might not feel like it, in urban areas in 2000, the number of days when air pollution was recorded as moderate or higher fell to 16 days on average per site, compared with 30 days in 1999 and 23 days in 1998. The figure for 1999 was higher partly because warmer weather meant higher ozone levels. Even in rural parts of the country, the figures showed an improvement – air pollution was recorded as moderate or higher on 25 days on average per site in 2000, compared with 48 in 1999. However, ACE's Joe Buchdahl is highly sceptical about these figures. 'The weather could have had an impact on the 2000 results,' he says. 'It rained a lot last year and there were relatively fewer days of sunlight, which speeds up the chemical reaction that produces low-level ozone.'

Other scientists and campaigners also point out that the reason nitrogen dioxide pollution, one of the main concerns in urban areas, has been reduced is because of the introduction of catalytic converters on vehicles in the 1990s and the compulsory cleanup of power stations. Additionally, legislation to combat acid rain has brought down sulphur dioxide levels. However, as the NSCA's Tim Brown points out, 'the big problem of road traffic has not been tackled effectively. Individual vehicles are cleaner, but more traffic equals more pollution.'

SHOCKING FACT NO 3: Traffic is expected to grow by half as much again from 1998–2026

This isn't campaign sensationalism, these are Government figures that don't somehow square up with shocking fact no 2. According to Transport 2000, the good air-quality figures have come through technical advances, not a reduction in traffic. But new technologies, such as cleaner engine fuels, are not enough in themselves to combat pollution from growing traffic. A Transport 2000 spokesman warns: 'Britain is falling short of other EU countries because we are still stuck in the 'car is best' phase that we entered in the 1980s, and haven't developed real alternatives in public transport or encouraged walking or cycling.'

The Government's new Department of Environment, Food and Rural Affairs is responsible for delivery on air quality. However, it is local authorities that have to put together local action plans to tackle traffic and it will be another year before we know whether these action plans are working. Brown says the Government is scared of looking anti-car. 'There was nothing on air pollution in the **Queen's Speech**. But we don't need new legislation, although roadside emission tests and stop checks on vehicle exhausts would be a good idea. We need alternatives to car use: it is too easy and cheap to use them now,' he says.

Some cities are striving to clean up their act – London, Nottingham, Bristol and York are exploring low-emission zones that would allow only cleaner vehicles to enter, congestion charging and other car-reduction measures.

However, Joe Buchdahl believes we need to take more personal responsibility. 'People need to be aware that they are part of the problem and also part of the solution,' he says. 'Air pollution in the developed world has become a personal problem because industrial pollution is falling all the time, but pollution from transport is increasing. Not enough is being done to encourage a sense of responsibility. It's like when you are in a traffic jam, it is always everyone else's fault, never your own.'

Focus, **September 2001**

Queen's Speech: a speech read out by the Queen at the opening of Parliament, setting out the government's aims and intentions for the coming session

Activities

Writing to inform

1 Before you start to read extracts from the above list, complete the following exercises.

   a Read the passage below, which has been written in the past tense. As you read, note down all the verbs.

> *If you followed the stream, you soon arrived at a small wood which grew on the left-hand side. Many different kinds of birds nested there, while rabbits, voles, foxes and badgers all made their homes in the undergrowth. It was well worth pausing for a while and sitting quietly to watch the wildlife before pressing on downstream.*

   b Re-write this passage in the present tense.

2 a As you read the extracts from the above list, note down anything that gives you an idea what kind of readers they have been written for.

   b With a partner or in a small group, select one extract you have read. Discuss your findings, using references to and quotations from the extract to back up your point of view.

   c On your own, write a short paragraph saying who you think the extracts you have read have been written for. Give at least three quotations from these extracts to back up your statements.

3 After reading and studying some or all of these extracts, write about the area in which you live to inform an exchange student who has come to stay with you from abroad. In your writing you must:

- use the present tense
- link your sentences and paragraphs clearly
- write appropriately for someone of your own age, but whom you have not met.

Writing to explain

1 Before you start to read extracts from the above list, complete the following exercises.

   a Make a flowchart of the actions you need to undertake to get and eat a school dinner from the moment the lunchtime bell goes until the moment you finish eating.

   b Using your flowchart as a plan, write a clear explanation of the procedures you need to follow to have a school dinner as if you were writing to explain the procedures to someone who is new to your school.

2 a As you read the extracts from the above list, note down the main points.

   b With a partner or in a small group, select one extract you have all read. Discuss your findings and put together a final list of the main points that you can all agree on.

c   On your own, write out your list as a flowchart. Include a short quotation from the extract for each main point.

3   After reading and studying some or all of the extracts listed on page 124, imagine you are walking quietly home from school one day when you meet a friendly extraterrestrial. You invite him home with you and offer him tea, only to discover he has no idea how to make, or eat, a sandwich. Write an explanation of how he can do this. In your explanation you must:

* organise the order in which the actions need to take place clearly
* make sure that each point of the explanation is clear.

Writing to describe

Extract 2.1:	David Beckham – Football, Fame and Fortune	(page 72)
Extract 2.7:	Orienteering	(page 103)
Extract 2.9:	With Austrian Cavalry on the Eastern Front	(page 108)
Extract 2.10:	Soaking in Port Sunlight	(page 111)
Extract 2.11:	Visiting Hiroshima	(page 117)

1   Before you start to read extracts from the above list, complete the following exercises.

a   Work with a partner to note down three or four important positive things about him or her (for example, how s/he looks, or things s/he does or says).

b   Working on your own, write a brief description of your partner without using his or her name (and, if possible, without giving away the person's gender). Copy out your description on a small sheet of paper.

c   Working as a class, collect in everybody's descriptions, mix them up and read them out. Try to identify each of the people as the descriptions are read aloud. How many people can be identified accurately just from these three or four details?

2 a   As you read the extracts listed on page 125, pay particular attention to the details the writers give to make their descriptions clear and vivid. Note down the details that seem to you to be particularly important.

b   With a partner or in a small group, select one extract you have read. Discuss your findings and each compile a final list of all the details the writer has included.

c   On your own, write five questions you would like to ask the writer to help you to understand even better the emotions, actions or places he or she has described.

3   After reading and studying some or all of the extracts listed on page 125, write a description of a place you know well. Make it as clear and vivid as you can, so that your reader will be able to picture it clearly and understand how you feel about it.

Section 3
Writing to persuade, argue, advise

The writers in this section all have a particular standpoint, a view, a belief about what they are writing about. Some of them are trying to persuade their readers to share their point of view, others are trying to argue the case for their point of view and show why they believe they are right, while yet others are trying to advise their readers about how to behave in particular situations. But they are all speaking as specialists and sharing their inside understanding with their readers.

Extract 3.1

In 1989, a group of writers got together to help with the charity fund-raiser Comic Relief by publishing a book giving advice to children on 'how to survive at school'. In this passage, they suggest ways of coping with homework, lessons and free periods.

Incredibly Naughty Ways to Survive Work and Lessons at School

One of the smelliest things about school – apart from drains, PE and macaroni cheese – must be all the work and lessons you have to do.

The two things, though, which are absolutely the worst are science and writing essays about what we did on our holidays. We got so fed up copying out the same old rubbish, we invented some new rubbish!

William and Jemima Brat's instant what-we-did-on-our-holidays essay

Simply copy out this essay filling in the gaps with a word of your choice from the appropriate list. The result will be brilliant and win you top marks – or 500 lines . . .

[a]	[b]	[c]	[d]
summer	Blackpool	family	a boarding house
Xmas	Transylvania	suitcase	a shed
Easter	The Amazon jungle	pet fish	Dracula's Castle
Hallowe'en	The Post Office	killer zombie	a slime pit

[e]	[f]	[g]	[h]
camp bed	share	cousin	hot
bucket	eat	killer zombie	cold
bath of acid	empty	octopus	windy
dung heap	clean	teeth	wet

[i]	[j]	[k]	[l]
food	small	fun	swimming pool
beach	runny	trouble	roadworks
room	far from the toilet	laughs	zoo
car park	radioactive	injuries	funfair
bucket	full of jelly	boils	sewer outlet

[m]	[n]	[o]	[p]
Dad	water	experience	laugh
Mum	tiger's cage	holiday	fun
whelks	dodgems	Xmas	jelly
passers-by	path-of-a-steamroller	bucket	goat

[q]	[r]
had	soon
eaten	never
juggled	next year
disintegrated	when I get out of hospital

This . . . [a] . . . I went to . . . [b] . . . with my . . . [c] . . . . We stayed in . . . [d] . . . and I slept in a . . . [e] . . . which I had to . . . [f] . . . with my . . . [g] . . . .

The weather was very . . . [h] . . . and Dad complained about the . . . [i] . . . , which he said was too . . . [j] . . . .

We had a lot of . . . [k] . . . when we played at the . . . [l] . . . and we pushed . . . [m] . . . into the . . . [n] . . . .

It was a wonderful . . . [o] . . . and the best . . . [p] . . . I have ever . . . [q] . . . . I hope we go back there . . . [r] . . . .

Science is dull, dull, dull except when we do live experiments in the lab. Our fave is to put worms down the back of the School Swot's trousers and time how long it takes him to scream like a big sissy. There are loads of other ways to make a nuisance of yourself:

Experiments you CAN do in the school laboratory with out getting really bored
Using a clean test tube, an old lavatory roll and some fluffy bits from a stoat's belly-button, do the following experiments:

- Cross a PE teacher with an elephant to produce an elephant in a tracksuit who can't do joined-up writing.
- Set fire to the School Cook's chair – preferably with the School Cook sitting in it – to produce a sat-alight dish.
- Cross the School Bully with a mad squirrel and produce a complete and utter nutter.
- Try crossing the Cricket Coach with a lump of wood to come up with something completely batty.

Experiments you CANNOT do in the school science laboratory
For thousands of years scientists have tried to re-create the yellow gunge School Cook puts in our macaroni cheese. THIS IS EXTREMELY DANGEROUS AND MUST NOT UNDER ANY CIRCUMSTANCES BE ATTEMPTED BY UNQUALIFIED STUDENTS.

Of course all lessons are naff and boring unless you play the really BAD game William and I invented. It's the only thing known to Man and Woman to get you through double history:

The Brat anti-boredom technique
With your snotty little friends, think up a completely ridiculous word before Teach arrives. The idea is to make Teach say the chosen word before the end of the lesson.

For example, if it's history you might choose 'washing machine' and the lesson might go like this:

Teacher	After conquering Western Europe, Napoleon and his army set out east to conquer Russia . . .
You	Please, Miss? How did they keep their clothes clean on the march?
Teacher	They didn't.
Friend	You mean they wore dirty clothes?
Teacher	That's right.
Friend	Couldn't they have taken something along with them to clean the clothes with?
Teacher	I suppose they could [IRRITATED]. They probably had soap.
Friend	So they did them by hand?

Teacher	Yes, I suppose so. Anyway [ANNOYED], as I was saying, they marched from Paris . . .
You	Couldn't they have done them with something electrical?
Teacher	Oh, do stop talking nonsense Brat – I mean, you don't honestly think they carried washing machines with them, do you?!!!???

DING DING DING!!!!!

You win – start the next lesson with a new word.

Five ways to put a free period to good use
1 Call a meeting of the Escape Committee, and continue digging your tunnel.
2 Block up the staff-room door with a large object (e.g. school piano, elephant, **Russell Grant**), so that your next period will also be teacher-free.
3 Paint spots on your face, so teacher will send you home. (Don't do this if you've got one of those spotty young teachers, or he'll think you're making fun of him.)
4 Smear your exercise books with chicken giblets and tempt a stray dog to savage them, so you've an excuse for not handing in your homework.

Russell Grant: a television astrologer known for his rather large build

5 Do the 1,000,000 lines you've been given for trying the preceding 4 ruses in your last free period.

Huw Tristan Davies, Alan Rowe, Patrick Gallagher, Mark Rodgers, Ed McHenry, Michael Peek, Tony Husband and Kev F. Sutherland, *What a Comic Relief! The Incredibly Naughty Survive at School Handbook*

Extract 3.2

You can get help with all sorts of things on the web, including how to make option choices at school. Do you think the advice offered here is clear and helpful?

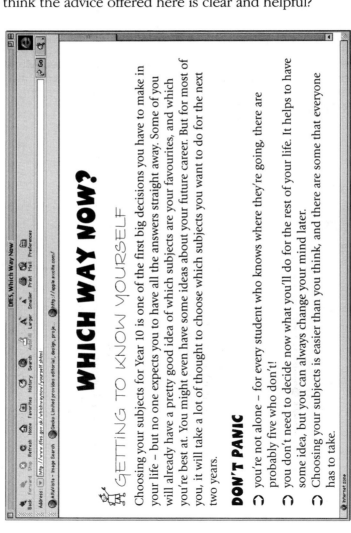

WHICH WAY NOW?

GETTING TO KNOW YOURSELF

Choosing your subjects for Year 10 is one of the first big decisions you have to make in your life – but no one expects you to have all the answers straight away. Some of you will already have a pretty good idea of which subjects are your favourites, and which you're best at. You might even have some ideas about your future career. But for most of you, it will take a lot of thought to choose which subjects you want to do for the next two years.

DON'T PANIC

○ you're not alone – for every student who knows where they're going, there are probably five who don't!

○ you don't need to decide now what you'll do for the rest of your life. It helps to have some idea, but you can always change your mind later.

○ Choosing your subjects is easier than you think, and there are some that everyone has to take.

Writing to persuade, argue, advise   135

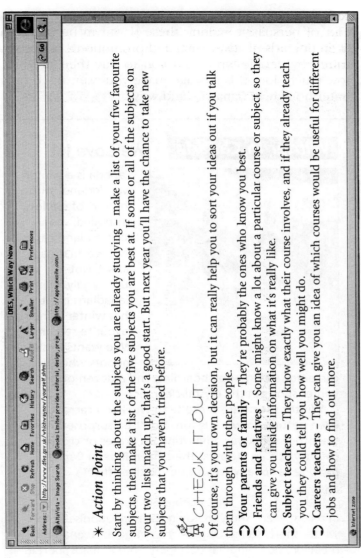

Action Point

Start by thinking about the subjects you are already studying – make a list of your five favourite subjects, then make a list of the five subjects you are best at. If some or all of the subjects on your two lists match up, that's a good start. But next year you'll have the chance to take new subjects that you haven't tried before.

CHECK IT OUT

Of course, it's your own decision, but it can really help you to sort your ideas out if you talk them through with other people.

- **Your parents or family** – They're probably the ones who know you best.
- **Friends and relatives** – Some might know a lot about a particular course or subject, so they can give you inside information on what it's really like.
- **Subject teachers** – They know exactly what their course involves, and if they already teach you they could tell you how well you might do.
- **Careers teachers** – They can give you an idea of which courses would be useful for different jobs and how to find out more.

www.dfes.gov.uk

.ract 3.3

.λ lot of persuasive writing these days can be found in different kinds of advertising and promotional material – written by people who want you to buy their product. How much does this passage make you want to go on a winter holiday in Canada – and why?

Winter in Canada – We Love It!

Canada is a winter wonderland, with the sort of endless, unspoiled, snow-covered landscapes that we all dream about. Not surprisingly, many Canadians insist that winter is their favourite season. Who wants to stay indoors when you can enjoy skiing, snowboarding and a dozen other winter sports in the crystal-clear air?

Winter sports are more than weekend recreation: even getting to work is fun. Don't be surprised if you see office workers commuting on skates or cross-country skis. In Ottawa, the frozen Rideau Canal provides a speedy way to get to the office!

Catching air

In recent years, snowboarding has revolutionised the winter sports scene. Originally a symbol of teenage rebellion, boarding has developed into a major sport in its own right. What's more, older folk (such as parents!)

are trying it out … and loving it! Like surfing on snow, boarding is fast and exciting, and easier to learn than skiing. Three days of lessons should see you well away, and resorts all over Canada cater for boarders.

Have skis – will travel

Canadians keep cross-country skis propped up and ready by the back door. Anywhere and everywhere is ideal for cross-country, or Nordic, skiing. Choose from urban parks, golf courses, country fields, frozen lakes or any of the thousands of marked trails. You can also enjoy cross-country skiing along the lower slopes of the Rockies in Alberta, across vast expanses of open prairie in Saskatchewan and Manitoba, through unspoiled forests in Ontario and from one country inn to the next in Quebec. In Nova Scotia, cross-country trails weave through woodlands, highlands and open fields, while in New Brunswick the extensive network of trails winds through several provincial parks. In the very far north, glaciers provide year round skiing on Nunavut's Baffin Island! Some resorts are dedicated exclusively to the sport, but nowadays, many of the downhill skiing resorts also prepare cross-country routes along their valleys.

Best foot forward

If you like to walk, then you must try snowshoes. You might feel clumsy wearing them at first, but once you've mastered the technique, enthusiasts say it's like walking on clouds. Snowshoes were invented for getting around in the winter without sinking into deep snow. The originals were made of wood and rawhide webbing, and shaped like tennis racquets. Centuries later, this is still the preferred design, though plastic models are also popular. You can hire them for half an hour, half a day, or longer.

Fun on four legs

If you prefer to get around under someone (or something) else's steam, nothing beats travelling in an old-fashioned horse-drawn sleigh ... it really is romantic!

Or how about dog sledding? The dogs are generally northern breeds like Alaskan Malamute or Siberian and Alaskan Huskies. The driver is still known as the 'musher', derived from the French 'marchez!' (go!), which the French Canadians shout at their dog teams. English settlers reduced this to 'Mush!'. By dogsled, you can travel up to 30 miles a day. When rivers and lakes are frozen over, this can be not just the best, but the only way to get around. In Alberta, there's a variation called ski-joring. Just hook yourself up to a sturdy sled dog and let him/her pull you on skis along cross-country ski trails ... like water-skiing on snow!

High speed thrills

The fastest way (and still an authentically Canadian way) to get around in winter is by snowmobile. Back in 1922, Joseph-Armand Bombardier, a mechanic living in Quebec's Eastern Townships, developed a propeller-driven sled. That was the grand-daddy of today's high-tech mean machines. Apart from being an essential means of getting around, especially in remote areas, snowmobiles are pure fun. Not surprisingly, Quebec has a huge network of 16,000 snowmobile trails reaching almost every corner of the province. In New Brunswick, if you visit the St John River area, you can retrace old trails that were made by natives and early settlers long before the invention of the snowmobiles.

Extract 3.4
This passage is taken from a book published by The Pony Club, an association that encourages riding for young children. At a time when the pastime of hunting animals is increasingly being called into question (and may even be made illegal), it is interesting to read the view of an organisation that takes such practices for granted. Here The Pony Club is giving advice to young people who are going fox hunting.

Going Fox Hunting

Preparation and turnout
Lack of preparation before a day's hunting can bring discomfort and disappointment: causing you to arrive late at the meet and not being able to find hounds, for example; or to lose a shoe at the beginning of the day.

The day before hunting it is important to check that your pony is fit, well shod, and ready at hand for the morning. If it is possible to keep a grass-kept pony in the night before, you will be saved a lot of work tidying him up. Check that your tack is clean and safe. As ponies often get excited out hunting, causing them to pull much harder than they would normally, a stronger bit may be needed.

If you can, use rubber-covered reins, which are much easier to grip, especially in wet weather on a sweaty pony.

Flashy items of tack – such as coloured browbands or sheepskin nosebands – have no place in the hunting field.

Girth buckles should be checked for wear. Stirrup irons should be large enough not to catch the foot. A **numnah** is useful to prevent chafing on a fat pony during a long day; the dark-coloured, linen-lined variety are easier to keep clean.

A plaited pony looks smart, but this is not essential, as long as the mane is neatly pulled and the tail is **banged** at a reasonable length.

Check the amount of time that you will need to set off in the morning in order to arrive at least five minutes before the advertised hour of the meet. Allow plenty of time beforehand to get your pony ready and to have breakfast. Don't forget to take some sandwiches and/or a chocolate bar.

Correct dress
- Pony Club Members should wear only those hats marked with PAS 015 (with BSI kitemark or SEI), EN1384 (with BSI kitemark or SEI) and ASTM F1163 (with SEI), with a dark blue or black cover, or a well-fitted hunting cap with safety harness. The hat should be worn straight, and girls should make sure that they have no hair showing at the front of the hat and that hair at the back is secured in a net.
- A tweed jacket should be worn with a collar and tie or a collarless shirt with a white or dark-spotted

numnah: saddle-cloth or horse blanket (numnah comes from a Hindi word, which was brought into English by soldiers and civil servants working in India when it was part of the British Empire; some other Hindi words that have become part of the English language are 'pyjamas', 'bungalow' and 'khaki')
banged: cut short

hunting tie (otherwise known as a 'stock'). This should be held in place with a plain bar tie pin.

- Earrings, however small, should never be worn out hunting, as they can get caught in branches of trees or in your chinstrap, and can cause very nasty injuries to your ears.
- Fawn jodhpurs with black or brown jodhpur boots should be worn. Older children can wear fawn breeches and riding boots. The boots, even rubber ones, should be well polished, and spurs should be worn high on the seam of the boot above the heel with the blunt end pointing downwards.
- Gloves which do not become slippery when wet are essential; woollen or string ones are recommended.
- A hunting whip with thong and lash is both correct and practical. The thong can be used to prevent hounds from getting under your pony, and the handle is invaluable for opening and shutting gates.

The above dress is correct until you are twenty-one or unless you have been awarded the Hunt button by the Master. Being given the button acknowledges that you are a member of the Hunt; you can now also wear the Hunt collar (if there is a special one) on your black coat. Full details of hunting dress for adults and children are given in The Pony Club publication, *Correct Dress for Riding*.

Rules for riding to hounds
- When you move off from the meet into the hunting field your object should be to ride to hounds so that you can see and hear them hunting the fox.

- Never forget that wherever you are hunting you are the guest of the local farmer or landowner, and that you are very lucky indeed to be able to have access to private land.
- Because of modern farming techniques, there may well be special routes across certain farms which have been agreed between the farmer and the Hunt. The Field Master will be well acquainted with these routes, and it is important for you to be alert and to follow any instructions which he gives.
- When hounds are **drawing**, keep quiet and pay careful attention.
- Do not let your pony upset others by fussing or knocking into them. That is the way to get kicked. If your pony is liable to kick, keep him well out of the way. A pony who *habitually* kicks should not be taken hunting.
- When hounds are running, do not bump or cut in on other riders at gateways or jumps. If your pony should stop at a jump, take him back and let everyone else go before you try again.
- When you are told to keep in single file around the edge of cultivated land – such as corn or young grass – make sure that you keep in tight to the edge. This means round the corners as well! Also, keep your distance, and do not tread on the heels of the horse in front, which can cause a nasty injury.
- Jump off your pony quickly to help open or shut a gate.

---

drawing: searching for the fox's scent

- Report any damage, such as a broken fence, to the Master or the Secretary.
- Always pass on the message to shut a gate ('Gate, please') loudly and clearly. If there is no one immediately behind you, either wait for someone, or shut the gate yourself. Never gallop off and leave someone to shut a gate on their own. Always wait and help.
- Always *ride round* a herd of cattle or a flock of sheep. Never alarm them by galloping through them.
- Always make way for the Master or hunt staff, and let other people know by calling 'Master on the left' or 'Huntsman on the right'. If hounds come past you in a lane or a ride, always turn your pony's head towards them and hold the thong of your hunting whip out to prevent them getting under your pony's feet. This is important – even if you do not think your pony will kick.
- Never gallop your pony unnecessarily, he may need energy later. Give him an easy time when climbing uphill or in heavy going.
- Do not gallop through deep, muddy gateways. Always slow up and collect your pony, as you could have a nasty fall.
- When possible, say 'Good night' and 'Thank you' to the Master and huntsman before going home.

Alastair Jackson, *Hunting*

Extract 3.5
Leslie Scrase has published several books and articles
about Humanism, a belief that holds there is nothing after
death, and that the important thing is to live your life well
and thoughtfully. Here he gives advice on how to cope
with the death of a loved one.

Coping with Death:
Life After Bereavement

When people are overwhelmed by their grief it is hard
for them to do anything more than grasp emotional
comfort from those who are close to them. The best
comfort just then is often to have someone sit with you
and hold your hand; or to be held in the arms of
someone who loves you. But once the mind begins to
function again, then all kinds of comfort can be found.
We seek it within our own human situation. Because we
do, it will never be quite the same twice, because no two
human situations are the same.

There is often comfort to be found in the death itself. We
speak sometimes of a 'merciful release'. And sometimes
we can find comfort where none seems possible. I
remember sitting with a young Irish girl, widowed after one
month of marriage. Her husband had been a soldier. Early
one morning he was driving to his barracks, skidded on
black ice, and was killed in the crash. I sat with his widow,
holding her hand and feeling absolutely useless. As we sat
quietly together she said two things:

'Well at least he never killed anybody else in his life,'
and 'I've been his wife. No one can ever take that away
from me.'

She was beginning to use her mind to find her own comfort. In the end that is what we all have to do. Sometimes when we want to comfort bereaved people we wonder what we can possibly say that will help. But it is not so much what we say as what we hear that matters. Our primary task is to listen and to act as a sounding board. We enable people to express their grief and to get it out of their system – at least for the moment. We also help them to clutch at the first straws of comfort that come to their minds. If we are listening carefully enough, we can make the most of those straws.

And is that all?

Of course not. But it takes time to discover more lasting comfort.

It takes time to get the misery out of our system. And this is where an understanding friend can often be of immense help. Two or three weeks after the funeral the subject of the death in the family suddenly becomes **tabu**. No one refers to the person who has died because no one wants to open up old sores. And there we are bottling it all up with no one to talk to; no one to share what we are feeling. It is then that we need someone to come to us and make the first move:

'Do you want to talk about it?'

And it all pours out and it is such a relief. And we know that whenever we want to, here is a person who will listen as we talk about our loved one to our heart's content . . .

It also takes time to discover the comfort of memory. Nowadays adult families are often scattered all over the world so that we see each other rarely. Of course we can write letters. But most of us are bad correspondents. And we can telephone – but most of us have half a thought for the size of our telephone bill. Cheapest of all: we can think about our loved ones. In point of fact

---

tabu: something sacred that must not be touched or mentioned we can't avoid it. A thousand and one things will bring them to mind.

Exactly the same is true of those who have died. A thousand and one things will bring them to mind.

If we are part of a family we will often 'see' our loved ones again in gestures, expressions and ways of speaking and acting that have been passed on. And there are so many trivial things in life that bring our loved ones back to us vividly. Every time I put my foot on a chair to tie up my shoelace, I can hear mother ticking my father off for the same crime.

What's more: memory doesn't fade. I was always told that it did. But my own experience is that the more you loved someone, the more their memory stays fresh and vivid. If that can be poignant it can also be joyful – and if you have let your loved one go, the poignancy fades but the joy continues.

All these kinds of comfort involve looking back and dwelling in the past. Is that all there is for us? Is there no life after bereavement? When we have lost our nearest and dearest is there any reason for us to go on living?

At first we may do little more than find comfort for today and a reason for tomorrow. But even that is enough to enable us to go with life. The rest is partly a matter of time and partly a matter of will and determination.

Earlier in this chapter I mentioned the Irish girl who lost her husband. She was in her twenties when he died. It is obvious that someone in her position can start life again; create a new life; find a new love and build a new joy.

But what about those who are bereaved at the other end of life?

For me, it will always be my father who points the way. My mother died when they were both in their mid-eighties. They had celebrated their diamond wedding anniversary a year before she died. For the last few years of her life she had been crippled with arthritis and heavily dependent upon my father. She had been his life. When she died I expected him to follow.

Just how he summoned up the will and energy to begin again I don't know. But he did. He began to do all those things he had told us that he wanted to do. I had never believed him. I thought that mother was his excuse for not doing them. But I was wrong. He built a new life for himself to such purpose that people called him 'the happiest man in Rustington'.

It is true that he had many things going for him – supremely: health and energy. But I am convinced that more than anything else it was his attitude of mind that enabled him to triumph over his grief and begin again so successfully . . .

When the **humanist** is bereaved, have we nothing to offer?

Of course we have.

There are the comforts the mind discovers in the midst of our bereavement. There are the comforts provided by the surrounding circle of friends and loved ones. There are the ongoing comforts of joyful and amusing memories. There is the continuing life of our loved one in the lives of the rest of the family – the children and grandchildren – and in the things our loved one has done.

But the humanist whose mind is set so firmly on this world and this life, should also be able to turn without any lack of respect or feeling, firmly from the past. Lovingly we leave the past behind and set about the task of creating our own new future, however long or short that may be.

We sit down to dinner with my mother-in-law. When we have finished she is only half-way through. How sad it

---

humanist: follower of a system of thought that does not believe in God, but concentrates on human interests and behaviour

would be if she failed to enjoy the rest of her meal just because we had finished. When our loved ones have completed their feast of life we can learn to go on to enjoy what is left of our own.

Leslie Scrase, from *Coping With Death, a booklet for the bereaved and those who try to help them*

Extract 3.6
Lieutenant Colonel Peter Boxhall is an explorer, writer and student of the Arabic language and culture. He has spent a long time working in different Arab countries. In this extract from *The Traveller's Handbook*, he gives advice to travellers visiting Muslim countries.

Respecting Islam

Like any nation with an important history, the Arab people are proud of their past. Not only because of an empire which once stretched from the far reaches of China to the gates of France, or their many great philosophers, scientists, seafarers, soldiers and traders, but because they are one people, sharing a common language and culture and following the same religion, which has become an integral part of their lives and behaviour.

Language
Arabic is a difficult language for us to learn, but it is a beautiful, expressive one, which, in the early days of Islam, came to incorporate all the permissible culture, literature and poetry of Arab society. Small West African children sitting under cola trees write their Koranic lessons on wooden boards, infant Yemenis learn and chant in unison *suras* of the Holy Book, school competitions are held perennially in the Kingdom of Saudi Arabia and elsewhere to judge the students' memory and knowledge of their written religion.

So, as in any foreign environment, the traveller would do well to try and learn some Arabic. For without the greetings, the enquiries, the pleasantries of everyday conversation and the ability to purchase one's requirements, many of the benefits and pleasures of travel are **foregone**. Best, too, to learn classical (Koranic) Arabic, which is understood throughout the Arabic-speaking world (although the further away one is from the Arabian Peninsula in, for example, the Mahgreb countries of Morocco, Tunisia and Algeria, the more difficult it is to comprehend the dialectal replies one receives).

Not long ago, before the advent of oil, when one travelled in the harsh environment of the Arabian Desert, the warlike, nomadic Bedu tribes would, if they saw you came in peace, greet you with *salaam alaikum* and afford you the hospitality of their tents. If 'bread and salt' were offered to you, you were 'on their face'; inviolate, protected, a welcome guest for as long as you wished to stay. *Baiti baitak* (my house is your house) was the sentiment being expressed. This generous, hospitable principle still prevails throughout the Arab world.

Social conventions

Baiti baitak is the greatest courtesy. Do not, however, be critical or admiring of the furniture in the house. If you admire the material things, your

---

foregone: missed

hospitable host may feel impelled to give you the object of your admiration . . .

If it is an old-style house, you must always take your shoes off, and may be expected to sit on the floor supported by cushions. Then all manner of unfamiliar, exotic dishes may be served. If it is painful to plunge your fingers into a steaming mound of rice, and difficult to eat what are locally considered to be the choice pieces of meat, forget your inhibitions and thin skin, eat everything you are offered with your right hand and at least appear to enjoy it. Remember, your host is probably offering you the best, sometimes the last remaining provisions in his house . . .

Coffee and tea are the habitual refreshments: in Saudi Arabia, as was the custom in my municipal office, the small handle-less cups of *qushr* are poured from the straw-filled beak of a brass coffee pot. 'Arabian coffee' is also famous: almost half coffee powder, half sugar. One should only drink half or two-thirds, however, and if you are served a glass of cold water with it, remember that an Arab will normally drink the water first (to quench his thirst) then the coffee so that the taste of this valued beverage may continue to linger in the mouth.

In North Africa, tea is a more customary drink. Tea *nuss wa nuss* with milk in Sudan, for example; tea in small glasses with mint in the Mahgreb; even tea with nuts in Libya. Whoever was it said that the English are the world's greatest tea drinkers? Visiting the Sanussi tribe in Libya, I once had to drink 32 glasses of tea in the course of a morning. The tea-maker, as with the Arabian coffee-maker, is greatly respected for his art.

Dress

In most of the Arab world, normal European-type dress is appropriate, but it should be modest in appearance. Again if, as we should do, we take notice of Arab custom, which is based on sound common sense, we might do well to remember that in hot, dusty conditions, the Bedu put on clothes to protect themselves against the elements, not take them off, as we Westerners do.

Religion

The final, and perhaps most important piece of advice I can offer to the traveller is to repeat the need to respect Islam. The majority of Arabs are Muslim, and Islam represents their religion and their way of life, as well as their guidance for moral and social behaviour. In the same sense that Muslims are exhorted (in the *Koran*) to be compassionate towards the non-believer (and to widows, orphans and the sick), so too should we respect the 'Faithful'. Sometimes one may meet religious fanatics, openly hostile, but it is rare to do so and I can only recall, in my many years in Arab countries, one such occasion. Some schoolboys in south Algeria enquired why, if I spoke Arabic, I was not a Muslim, and, on hearing my answer, responded: *'Inta timshi fi'n nar'* (You will walk in the fires of Hell).

In some countries you can go into mosques when prayers are not in progress, in others entry is forbidden altogether. Always ask for permission to photograph mosques and (in the stricter countries) women, old men and children.

Respect, too, the various religious occasions and that all-important month-long fast of Ramadan. My Yemeni doctors and nurses all observed Ramadan, so one year I joined them, to see exactly what an ordeal it was for them. Thereafter, my admiration for them, and for all others who keep the fast, was unbounded, and I certainly do not think we should exacerbate the situation in this difficult period by smoking, eating or drinking in public.

Ahlan wa sahlan: welcome! You will hear the expression often in the Arab world, and it will be sincerely meant.

Peter Boxhall, from *The Traveller's Handbook*, ed. Jonathan Lorie

Extract 3.7

Peter Bruggen is a psychiatrist and Charles O'Brian is a lecturer in social work, both specialising in the difficulties of young adults. Realising through their work that there were a lot of problems they encountered again and again, they decided to write a book about the most common difficulties arising in adolescence, and how to deal with them. Here they suggest ways of coping with problem children – and problem parents . . .

Surviving Adolescence

On any number of occasions in our own lives we have achieved things that in the past we would have thought possible only by waving a magic wand. When we were adolescents we would not have predicted that we could have, nor dreamed that we would ever want, our present jobs. Such jobs were not even in our own minds until we were about 30. Sometimes we seem to have planned most carefully the course of events and feel pleased by the achievement. Sometimes it seems as if it just 'happened' and we feel lucky. Which is the right feeling to have? A lot of the time we find it difficult to believe that we are writing this book and we wonder how long it will take us to accept or really believe that it has been published. We sometimes wonder how we have achieved all this and by what criteria we measure it. As for the sense of achievement – how do we grade ours compared with that experienced by, say, the novelist **Christie Brown**,

Christie Brown: a severely disabled Irish writer, who only had mobility in one foot; his life and achievements formed the basis for the film *My Left Foot*, starring Daniel Day Lewis

who typed using his toe, or our own feelings when we built our first sandcastle?

We both had grandmothers who told us not to cross our bridges until we came to them, but both of us, when we start a journey, try to find out where we might need a bridge. Some things we can plan at the start and some we leave until later. Others just seem to happen.

We decided to write this book because many parents had spoken to us about difficulties they had with their teenage children and many teenage children had spoken to us about the difficulties they had with their parents. In all our conversations with them, one often-repeated phrase was 'the harder I tried, the worse the problem got'. On the occasions when things started to get better it was usually when the people involved had started to do things in a different way; when they had thought of doing something differently; when a friend or relative or someone outside the immediate family had suggested something different; when they had got the idea from a film they had seen, or a television programme, or a book, or a conversation overheard in a bus, or sheer inspiration.

Very often, in the chronic problems in people's minds, they feel that they have tried everything that they can think of, but closer examination often shows that they have been trying to do the same thing in different ways. Very soon they start a self-perpetuating cycle and any attempted solution becomes the problem:

> The more you keep your room untidy as a response to your mother's nagging, the more she nags.
> The more you nag your son about his untidy room, the untidier it gets.

Adults and teenage children easily get caught up in the cycle of nagging and getting nagged. They find themselves caught: one side nagging the other because they do not listen and the other not listening because they are nagged. The more the nagging – an attempted solution to the not listening – the more children do not listen; and the more they do not listen – an attempted solution to the nagging – the more the parents nag. Both attempted solutions have become a problem.

'Very well,' you may say to us, 'but we have tried everything else. It just is very hard to get them to listen (or to stop nagging).' Yes, you may very well be right. We are not offering an easy or magic solution to every problem; we are simply suggesting that looking in a different direction may open things up.

Very often, for things to change for the better, people have to act or think differently. It is almost like seeing things through a different pair of eyes. Very often, things that seem the most crazy, unusual, or hard to bear, may be just the sort of thing that might bring a change. Because the chances are that it will not be 'more of the same'.

We think that this is such an important point that we are going to go over it yet again, from one of the points of view – that of the adults. Your children are not listening to you and so you nag them. Now you know that in order to get somebody to listen to you, you must first have their attention. There are many ways of doing this. When you find that your particular way of trying to get your children's attention is not working, try something different. For example, you tell your child to be in by 11 p.m. She does not come in until 1 a.m. You tell her off about it. She obviously does not listen to you because she keeps on doing it. Apparently the more you start acting the authoritarian parent the less notice is taken of you. In other cases, being the authoritarian parent and laying the law down in a heavy way may work very well, and if this works with your child then please continue it.

If being the heavy authoritarian parent is not working, however, then you may like to think of other ways to get your child's attention. One variant to 'You must come it at

11 o'clock or else' might be 'I should like you to come in at 11 o'clock but I don't expect you to take much notice of me, so goodbye.' We are pretty sure that the latter statement after a long run of the former is more likely to grab children's attention and get them to start listening to you. We hope that any difference in the relationship may help both of you to get what you want. Do remember that with even that little example there are so many different ways of saying the words. If you say it in your usual tone of voice for that sort of statement it then becomes what we have called 'doing the same things differently'.

Everybody has a particular way of seeing things, including what they see as a problem. People talk about their 'problem' and its effect on their lives rather than doing something different. They seem to prefer it that way, but we think that it is only an appearance. We think that by doing something different, no matter how small, at least a different view is obtained of the problem. With this different way of seeing it the talking may take on a different quality, particularly if it is about changes.

When examining the problem you have with your children, or with your parents, we suggest you think of three questions; they might bring up interesting answers.

1 What is the problem?
2 How is it a problem to you?
3 What are you trying to do about it?

Problem parents

Even the best organised who appear very self-sufficient and independent have parents on whom they depended. Most adolescents have parents who are alive and active during their adolescence, dead but never completely forgotten, or somewhere in between. It is often in our teenage years that suspicions about parents having faults become certainties. Their feet of clay are all too clear.

Those of you who are parents but who are reading this section, which is really designed for teenagers, may care to ask yourselves how much of what we are saying is still relevant to you as parents. We all go on having a bit of the teenager in us.

In teenage, boys and girls become more embarrassed by the presence of their parents, by meeting them in the street and their expectation to be introduced to friends. What do they do with them at parties? Worst of all may be when they come to school. The most caring, concerned parents who come to support their adolescent children or to question their teachers have no idea how embarrassing this may be for the adolescents themselves.

Part of the process of separation is starting to detach oneself from, and not identifying with, parents. A usual experience for teenagers is to wonder if they may have been adopted because 'it is difficult to see how parents like them can possibly have produced someone like me'.

An exercise which might be of interest is to ask your friends to write down some of your qualities and some of your parents' qualities and to see how many similarities there may be. A further exercise is to work towards a definition of perfect parents: write a list of properties that perfect parents would have. Ask yourself if you know any and also ask your friends how your parents measure up to this list.

A group exercise can be for adolescents to describe their parents as objectively as they can and to write this on paper or on the computer. The descriptions are shuffled in a hat and picked out. The task then is to try to identify which parents are which.

Perfection does not exist. It is only a standard made up by people by which they measure others. The differences, that is the imperfections, are the reality. The parents you have are the best you have got. If you are having difficulties with them, then all you have to learn is how to deal with them . . .

In talking to adolescents we have found that areas which particularly concern them about their parents are:

1 Adolescents feel that parents continue to treat them as if they were younger than they are. In their presence, the adolescents feel continually under pressure to be different or to meet a certain standard or to be compared with their friends. They are nagged and embarrassed by this.

2 Parents fail to recognise sufficiently the separateness of their adolescent children. That they may have their own friends and want to be with them and want to be with their friends' families.

3 Secrecy. Parents want to know everything. It is not that the teenager may have anything to hide but the teenager resents the feeling that everything must be known and shared.

Peter Bruggen and Charles O'Brian, *Surviving Adolescence: a handbook for adolescents and their parents*

Extract 3.8
This is an extract from an article published in a magazine called *NI*, or *New Internationalist*. The writers of the article put forward a case for demonstrating against what they see as the evil of global capitalism by clowning around. Do you find their argument convincing?

Resistance is the Secret of Joy

The **FBI** have added 'Carnival Against Capital' – the name given to many of the mass actions for international days of protest from London to Quebec – to its list of wanted terrorist groups.

But 'Carnival Against Capital' is not an organization. It is: a pink fairy; a pie in the face; a man in a dress; a fire juggler; a samba rhythm. It is a tactic, the incarnation of the *spirit* of contemporary resistance to global capitalism. And if the FBI wants to infiltrate this movement, it may have to do so wearing pink tutus.

Did the 'Tactical Frivolity' women dressed in outrageous pink dresses, wild wigs, nine-foot-high fan tails and feather dusters dancing towards lines of confused Czech police during the International Monetary Fund meetings in Prague pose a terrorist threat?

Did the teddy bears launched by a large medieval catapult at the six-kilometre fence surrounding the Free Trade Area of the Americas summit in Quebec City threaten the **hegemony** of the market economy?

FBI: Federal Bureau of Investigation, American security agency
hegemony: dominance

Will the comedy army of the 'White Overalls' movement, who wrap door mats and cardboard round themselves for protection and attempt to non-violently push through police lines with inner tubes for shields and water pistols, bring capitalism to its knees?

Perhaps the real threat is the irresistible appeal of carnival as a tactic and strategy of resistance. Its creativity is contagious and totally unpredictable. Anything can happen during carnival. World Trade Organization (WTO) meetings get shut down. The FBI knows this and they can see it spreading. Around the world a new spirit is reinventing tactics of resistance, rejecting the tedium of ritual marches from A to B, the **verbose** rallies where the party faithful listen passively to long speeches by 'leaders'.

---

verbose: wordy, here referring to the number of speeches given at traditional rallies

Spontaneity and pleasure are the order of the day. As someone said at the Festival of Resistance against the WTO in Seattle: 'Even if we are getting our asses kicked, we are having more fun than they are.'

For if resistance and rebellion are not fun, do not reflect the world we wish to create, we are merely replicating previous repressive struggles which postpone pleasure, along with racial and gender equality, until 'after the revolution'.

Carnival and revolution have identical goals: to invert the social order with joyous abandon and to celebrate our indestructible lust for life, a lust that capitalism tries so hard to destroy with its monotonous merry-go-round of work and consumerism. It creates a new world by turning the present one upside down. But as Eduardo Galeano shows us, we live in a world already turned on its head, a 'desolate, de-souled world that practices the superstitious worship of machines and the **idolatry** of arms, an upside-down world with its left on its right, its belly button on its backside, and its head where its feet should be'. It's a world where children work and don't play, where 'development' makes people poorer, where cars are in streets where people should be, where a tiny minority of the world consumes a majority of its resources. And, he asks: 'If the world is upside-down the way it is now, wouldn't we have to turn it over to get it to stand up straight?'

John Jordan and Jennifer Whitney, *New Internationalist* 338, September 2001

---

idolatry: worship of idols or 'false gods'

Extract 3.9
This is part of a speech given to a girls' school in 1914, just before the outbreak of the First World War. As you read it, think about what kind of life the speaker is recommending for girls and women. Do you think the same kind of advice would be given to girls today?

Romance: An Address to Girls

I wish to speak this afternoon on a subject not often, perhaps, dealt with by those that have the opportunity of addressing a girls' school – ROMANCE. The word is, indeed, familiar enough, though too often degraded; but the thing *itself* is beautiful in significance and wide in bearing, and so may justly claim a word or two on an occasion like the present.

Let us briefly consider the word in its true meaning. We could hardly define it more shortly than as *a story of adventure*. At any rate that will answer my purpose. 'Adventure' – the outgoing of the soul on its unknown quest; 'quest' – the search for the Ideal that lies behind and beyond our every-day experiences. There are many ways in which man's adventurous spirit may find a means of **attaining** the far-off goal of its hopes, many ways whereby the life of each, in its endless effort, can be touched to **fine issues**. In the depth of every young heart lies some secret of Romance; and the aim of all that is most precious in Education should be to awake that heart to be eager, in its strange voyage of discovery through Time, to unravel the mystery of the world, and

---

attaining: reaching
fine issues: excellent, worthwhile outcomes

to **wrest** an inner meaning from the simple, commonplace things about us. The important point to bear in mind is that every true and honest thing in life has its own romance, if only we look for it, and are patient and humble in our search . . .

The soul of all romance finds its centre in the home. Unselfishness, devotion, gentleness, patience, sympathy, endurance, – Home is the perfect seed-plot of all these most Christian virtues. Cherish then the Home. Who serves Home best, serves God best; who loves Home most, most loves God. That is the **creed** of all manly men and womanly women. The romance of Home never grows old. Other things may fail; but the idea of Home **abides** unchangeable, at once the pledge and foretaste of that Eternal Home where, in the fullness of time, we hope to gather.

We hear a good deal, in this dissatisfied and uneasy age, of what girls are to do. Surely their first duty, as it is their last and loveliest privilege, will be to make the Home a nursery-ground for all that is constant and beautiful and happy, – the thought of it a hope, the memory of it an inspiration.

A woman I know was once asked whether, like her husband, she ever wrote poetry. She modestly replied, 'No.' In the room where the question was asked sat a friend who, on hearing it, quietly remarked: 'She lives the poetry she never writes.' It was the most exquisite compliment I ever heard paid; and it happened to be true. That woman had written something that the world would not willingly let die; she had written the true Romance.

E.H. Blakeney, *Romance: An Address to Girls*

---

wrest: tear, extract
creed: belief, faith
abides: stays, remains

Extract 3.10
Bertrand Russell was a philosopher and mathematician who was opposed to war. He had been a Conscientious Objector in the First World War – refusing to fight on grounds of conscience – and was profoundly disturbed by the possibility of nuclear war between America and the then Soviet Union during the 1950s and 1960s. Here he tries to put a case for peace.

Some Necessary Changes in Outlook

If the **Great Powers** can reach agreement that war is no longer to be an **instrument of policy**, one of the things that will have to be changed is education. Education in most countries is mainly in the hands of the national State and, therefore, tends to teach an outlook which is considered to be in the interests of the State concerned. It has not been thought, hitherto, that the interests of one State coincided with those of another. Nor, indeed, has this been true always, or even usually, in former times. It is the development of modern techniques, and, more especially, of nuclear weapons, that has made armed contests between States **futile** and has brought about an identity of interest between different countries far surpassing what was true at any earlier time. It follows that it is no longer to the interest of any country to emphasize its superiority to other countries or to cause

---

Great Powers: the most powerful countries in the world
instrument of policy: a way of acting to achieve a desired end
futile: useless

its boys and girls to believe it **invincible** in war. Nor is it a good thing to present martial glory as what is, above all things, to be admired.

It is especially in the teaching of history that changes are called for. This applies not only in the lower grades, but just as much in the highest academic teaching. **Hegel**, who announced that he had surveyed all human history, picked out three individuals as having the most outstanding merit. They were **Alexander, Caesar and Napoleon**. His academic successors in his own country were more nationalistic and preferred German heroes, while French boys were being taught that heroism is French, and English boys, that it is English. This sort of thing will have to cease. I suggested long ago, though with no hope that the suggestion would be adopted, that in every country the history of that country should be taught from books written by foreigners. No doubt such books would have a bias, but it would be opposed by an opposite bias in the pupils, and the outcome might be fairly just.

But it is not only history that needs to be differently taught. Everything (except, perhaps, arithmetic) should be taught as part of the progress of Man, and as a series of steps in the conquest of obstacles with which he has been faced and is still faced. There is a danger that, in ceasing to emphasize wars, teaching will cease to be exciting, but this danger can be entirely avoided by emphasizing exciting contests with difficulties and dangers other than those of war.

There are, one may say, three great spheres of contest involved in the gradual approach of man towards

---

invincible: cannot be beaten
Hegel: very influential late eighteenth-century German thinker
Alexander, Caesar and Napoleon: Alexander the Great, Julius Caesar and Napoleon Bonaparte, all great generals from different countries (Greece, Rome and France respectively)

wisdom. There are the contests with nature, the contests between men, and the contests within a man's own self. Each of these has its own history and its own importance.

The contests with nature, which begin with the problem of securing food, lead on, step by step, to the scientific understanding of natural processes and the technical power of utilizing sources of energy. It is in this sphere that man's greatest triumphs have hitherto been won, and it is likely that even greater triumphs will be achieved in the not very distant future. The story of man's increasing mastery over nature is inherently exciting, and is felt to be so by the young. To this kind of contest there is no limit. Each victory is only a **prelude** to another, and no boundaries can be set to rational hope.

The second kind of conflict, namely, that of men with other men, when it consists of armed combat between groups, is the one with which we have been especially concerned in this book. It is one which, on any rational survey, must be ended if human progress is to continue. I am not contending, as a full-fledged pacifist might, that contests between different groups of men have never in the past served a useful purpose. I do not think that this would be true. It has happened over and over again that barbarians have descended from the mountains upon fruitful plains and civilized cities and have done vast damage before civilized forces could curb their destructive vigour. But the increased area occupied by civilized men and the increased power which modern weapons have conferred upon them, has reduced to very small proportions the danger of such cataclysms as the destruction of the Roman Empire by the barbarians. It is not now barbarians who constitute the danger. On the contrary, it is those who are in the forefront of civilization. It should be one of the tasks of education to make vivid

---

prelude: forerunner, something that goes before

in the minds of the young both the merits of a civilized way of life and the needless dangers to which it is exposed by the survival of competitive ideals which have become **archaic**.

In the great majority of human beings, there is, in addition to outer conflicts, an inner conflict between different impulses and desires which are not mutually compatible. Systems of morality are intended to deal with such conflicts and, to a certain degree, they are often successful. But I think that the changing conditions of human life make changes of moral outlook necessary from time to time. One such change, which is especially necessary at the present time, is that each individual should learn to view groups of human beings other than his own as possible co-operators, rather than as probable competitors. But this whole subject is a very large one, and to pursue it would take us too far from our central theme.

What the world most needs, in education as in other departments of human life, is the substitution of hope for fear, and the realization of the splendid thing that life may be if the human family co-operatively will permit itself to realize its best potentialities.

Bertrand Russell, *Common Sense and Nuclear Warfare*

---

archaic: old fashioned, out of date

Extract 3.11

In this passage, Chris Garratt, Mick Kidd and David Stafford poke fun at pretentious artists by suggesting ways of appearing to be a genius.

How To Be An Artistic Genius

We live in a media age. Image is everything. In the past genius could, perhaps, have passed muster on product alone, but even then a smart creator knew that a little enigma wouldn't come amiss.

You want to look modern, but not naff: intelligent, but with a hint of sassy. A visit to one of our stylists here at the Genius Foundation should clear up most of your problems.

The first thing they'll deal with is the hair. Beards are still essential for male artists of a certain age. A long white one for the ancient genius, a short goatee for the middle-aged young bohemian. Female poets too should work hard to cultivate a few wisps. The powdered wig may once have been *de rigueur* but the contemporary rug is a sure sign of artistic insecurity. Rather opt for baldness, it never did **Picasso** any harm ... Anyway, if you're a proper genius you should be wearing a hat. At the turn of the century it was briefly thought that imagination, like heat, could be lost through the skull. Although science has since discredited this theory, geniuses are superstitious folk, so, to be on the safe side, most wear hats in public, in

---

Picasso: Pablo Picasso, famous (bald) Spanish artist

private and in earnest. You'd be a fool not to do the same . . .

But more important than any other aspect of appearance is the *pose*. The genius should pose at all times, until no gesture or movement is ill-considered, but particular attention should be paid to the detail of posing when being photographed for a book jacket, album cover or exhibition catalogue. Pose, pose, pose and pose again . . . Practise at home. Position several mirrors in such a way that you can see yourself as others see you. Try the following poses until you have made each look at least partially convincing . . .

a) The 'lost in my own brilliance' stare

Hold the index finger flat against the side of the cheek, with the other fingers folded, their knuckles resting against the lower lip. Incline the head down (avoiding sideways tilt) at an angle of 33 degrees. (Get the angle right; any more and it will look as if you should be in intensive care, any less and it will look as if you've had an accident with the Superglue.) Make the eyes vacant. Frown slightly as if trying to pursue a thought too deep for meaning. Or smile grimly as if you've just observed an irony which nobody else could possibly understand.

b) The 'I refuse to let you see how sensitive I actually am' semi-crouch

Sit with your bottom on the very edge of a chair, leaning forward with your knees apart. Allow a couple of locks of your hair, if of an appropriate length, to fall forwards. Clench the hands between the knees until the knuckles show white. Tighten the lips. Stay in this position for a long time even though it makes you want to go to the toilet. The effect is also ruined if you fall off the chair.

c) The 'Oh my, Oh my, such a world, such a world, so much input, but I'm on top of it' wipe

Stand. Tilt the head forward. Run the fingers of both hands through the hair from the front to the back (if bald a moment or two's deep massage of the scalp can have the same effect). Take the hands all the way to the back of the neck and then round to the chin. Clench them, with thumbs beneath the chin and fingers above, head still down. Stay in this position for a few seconds, allowing a gleam of excitement to sparkle in your eyes. Then, suddenly, look up and say something – just one or two words, it doesn't matter which – in a foreign language.

Chris Garratt, Mick Kidd and David Stafford, *How To Be An Artistic Genius*

Extract 3.12

Brian Aldiss is a science-fiction writer who wrote the original story on which the Steven Spielberg film *AI* is based. Here he describes how the story was developed into a film, and how his views have changed over the years it took to move from book to screen. He does not agree with the view of robots the director Spielberg portrays in the film, arguing that Spielberg's view is wrongheaded. What are Brian Aldiss' objections?

LIKE HUMAN, LIKE MACHINE

I am standing under a tree, looking at a squirrel on a bough above my head. The squirrel is looking at me. Eventually it decides to leave and swarms away, its action like a trigger, its tail following the **parabola** of retreat.

It is a moment of mammal empathy between us, such as you would not enjoy with a crab or a slug. There is no doubt that the squirrel is aware, conscious, working out its next move. I myself have extended consciousness, can foresee my death and reflect on my birth and the birth of the Universe, which the squirrel cannot. But not even in my youth could I have nipped up a tree as deftly as that squirrel.

The question of extended consciousness, or EXTC – I take the expression from Antonio Damasio's study *The Feeling of What Happens* – remains unanswered: how did it develop, where is it centred, what advantages does it deliver beyond the core consciousness of the squirrel?

---

parabola: curved line

Such questions did not engage me deeply in 1969 when I wrote my story *Supertoys Last All Summer Long*. Life is one thing, art another. At that time, excited by the workings of early computers, I believed that much was possible. I even shared a then common belief that the human brain worked like a computer, and that dreams were probably the computer downloading at the end of the day.

It was not hard – particularly within the limits of a short story – to imagine a small android boy who had been programmed to believe himself a real boy, and to love his adopted human mother. In any case, the story was more about love and the inability to love than the progress of computer science. I felt more affection for David, the android, and his side-kick, Teddy, than did Monica Swinton, the boy's adopted mother.

When Stanley Kubrick bought my story in 1982, I encountered a director who believed that the human race was faulty and would be better replaced by a phylum of robots. We got on well, because I also believed humankind to be faulty, though I was less keen on the robot idea. I remembered that C.S. Lewis had said: 'Let's pray that the human race never escapes from Earth to spread its iniquity elsewhere.' Note that this did not stop him imagining the human race escaping to Mars and Venus. Art is one thing, life another.

Kubrick and I never managed to write a screenplay. Nor did the others who worked with him on the idea. When Kubrick died in 1999 his friend Steven Spielberg took over the work. More than thirty years after the story was published, the Kubrick/Spielberg film derived from it, *AI*, has reached the big screen. In the film, androids move and talk and make love. And David survives a thousand years under ice in New

York harbour. In the future, things are evidently built to last. Without wanting to give the plot away, Monica does get to love David, before doing a **Little Nell** on us and fading away.

Where does EXTC fit in with all this? Take a step back in time. After the fifth great extinction, the small creatures of the **Palaeocene** – inheritors of the vanished dinosaurian world – were able to proliferate. What slowly emerged from the havoc was the world we recognise, the world of palm trees, peregrines, parsnips and primates.

From those primates we have evolved, to struggle with insects and bacteria for ownership of the world. With the cooling of the Earth during the **Miocene**, grasslands and open spaces developed. The **Bovidae** came into their own – fortunately for early humans, who were going to need sheep and goats for clothing as well as nourishment when the Ice Age arrived. Fortunately, too, grass grows from its roots – when grazed, it rapidly regenerates itself. These accidents of nature favoured another accident of nature, human beings, as they stood up on their hind legs and learned to live and hunt in groups.

The **savannahs** suited them. Their nearest relations were probably left behind in the rainforests. Of course there was competition. But most other mammals – elephants being a notable exception – live solitary lives, much like our domestic cat. In family groups,

---

Little Nell: heroine of a novel by Charles Dickens who dies romantically
Palaeocene: one of the very early ages in earth's history
Miocene: an early stage in earth's history following the Palaeocene
Bovidae: grazing animals (from the Ancient Greek *Bos*, meaning 'ox')
savannahs: grasslands

information can be traded and the old protected and tended for the knowledge they have accumulated. By then the basic reflexes prevailing over all mammalian life – fear, aggression, sexual impulse, hunger – had been **tempered** by intelligence and curiosity. The **opposable thumb** permitted the making of tools, weapons and pots – and the holding of paints with which to adorn the cave.

All this we understand, together with the rapid growth of the brain that makes us distinctively human. It does not tell us when EXTC dawned. It seems that part of the mind is rooted in the system of non-conscious **neural** patterns operating in the body – the roots of a tree whose leaves provide the rustle of consciousness itself.

The larger brain that distinguishes us as a species comes with a price tag. It uses up much energy. It means that women in childbirth must eject that large cranium from their wombs. The head itself – that treasure-house – is vulnerable, as clearly acknowledged in the days of beheadings. Yet consciousness has not evolved for utilitarian reasons, that we might forge sharper axes.

EXTC adds to the pure biological enjoyment of being alive. It assures us that we are alive, while the squirrel is alive but cannot realise the fact. Perhaps the first woman, gazing one night into the fire she had managed to domesticate, saw something magical in the flames, banishing the darkness around her. A

---

tempered: improved, made stronger
opposable thumb: capable of being opposed to, or applied so as to meet, a finger, so making it possible to pick up and hold tools, weapons and so on
neural: nerve

tender imagining took root in her brain. She felt a prompting beyond the material. In that moment, she saw herself as a separate Self, and marvelled.

We have come to realise what a wonder our extended conscious minds are. Our perceptual world is filled unbidden with imagery, with memories of family, with fatuities, old tunes and lines of dialogue spoken or unspoken, with quotes, figures, expectations and jokes, with fantasies about the girl next door or the hooligans next door but one.

Indeed, our brains are better designed to fantasise than to think logically. Fantasising, daydreaming and storytelling give such pleasure. For logic, for reason – not for pleasure – we have to go to school. EXTC constantly needs its fortifications, and knowledge its disciplines.

We should be asking ourselves the following question: supposing we form collectively the solitary EXTC in the galaxy, faulty though that consciousness may be, what then are the implications of this solemn imposition upon us? None? Or many, still to be determined? A destiny too grand yet to be considered? The opening words of *Hamlet* are 'Who's there?' We have yet to work out the answer.

It may be that our human awareness is still a mere flicker in the night, yet to catch full fire. Possibly in later centuries our EXTC will blaze up, will come to full flower and scorch out these subversive imaginings. Evolution is not over. Indeed, it is more than probable that with time we will understand this marvellous elusive property, EXTC. Its definition may well lead us to a new science, where the celebrated gulf between classical physics and quantum levels is bridged.

But how to define EXTC? How to pin it down? We come back to Steven Spielberg's film. It begins well, with a group of scientists discussing problems of artificial intelligence, but soon abandons such tricky questions for the sake of drama. The film shows us androids with manufactured brains who are indistinguishable from humans. Artificial intelligence: it sounds so simple. We just need better, faster computers, and to circumvent several million years of evolution, and we are home and dry.

Brains are far more than computers, even forthcoming computers with carbon **nanotubes** in place of today's silicon-based semiconductors. Intelligence cannot exist without consciousness. Artificial consciousness: that sounds like a taller order, and indeed it is.

No doubt many viewers of Spielberg's blockbuster will become convinced that such developments are just around the corner. Dream on, I say. Art is one thing, life another. We are fully entitled in a fiction to imagine what we will. Such imaginings give pleasure, and perhaps further the cause, as undoubtedly they did in the first journeys to the Moon – the outcome not only of cold war politics but also of science fiction. But there's a clear distinction between fiction and hard fact.

So what I believed in 1969 is what I do not believe in 2001. Nor has the theme of the poor neglected boy the personal appeal it once possessed. My own frail EXTC and everyone else's have moved on. We know more than we did about both technology and the human brain. The brain proves to be more wonderful than the planet Mars, and certainly more full of life.

Brian Aldiss, *New Scientist*, 15 September 2001

---

nanotubes: microscopically small tubes

Activities

Writing to persuade

Extract 3.3: Winter in Canada –
           We Love It!   (page 136)
Extract 3.9: Romance: An Address to Girls (page 163)

1 Before you start to read extracts from the above list, complete the following exercises.

   a Read the passage below.

> *It was raining very hard. The leaves on the trees were tossing in the wind. The birds were finding it hard to keep a grip on the branches or to make their way through the gusty air. It was a perfect day for a walk.*

   b Now re-write the passage to persuade your reader that this was indeed the perfect weather for a walk. Use repetition and exaggeration to catch your reader's imagination. The first sentence has been done for you.

> *The glittering, sparkling raindrops were rushing, twisting, tumbling like so many diamonds tossed down from the stormy sky.*

2 **a** As you read the extracts from the above list, draw up two lists of your own:

- one headed 'Information', under which you should list the facts the writer is describing

- one headed 'Persuasive devices', under which you should list the phrases the writer uses to persuade the reader of the attractions of what is being described.

b With a partner or in a small group, select one extract you have read. Discuss your findings and compile a final list of the information and the persuasive devices used in the passage.

c On your own, write two or three paragraphs showing how the writer uses language to persuade the reader to share his or her point of view. Use evidence from the text to back up what you say.

3 After reading and studying some or all of the extracts listed on page 178, write a description of your school to persuade parents to send their children there. To make your description as persuasive as possible you should use:

- exaggeration
- repetition.

Writing to argue

Extract 3.8:   Resistance is the Secret of
                      Joy   (page 160)
Extract 3.10: Some Necessary Changes in
                      Outlook   (page 165)
Extract 3.12: Like Human, Like Machine (page 172)

1 Before you start to read extracts from the above list, complete the following exercises.

a Choose a topic that interests you, such as animal rights, education or sports development. Whatever you choose, it must be a topic on which there are two opposing points of view.

b Research your topic using books, magazines, encyclopaedias and the Internet.

   c Note down evidence to support your own views.

   d Write a short argument putting forward your point of view on your chosen topic, using evidence from your research to back up your statements.

2 **a** As you read the extracts from the list on page 179, make notes on exactly what the writers are saying, what points of view they are expressing and what evidence they are using to back up their points of view.

   b With a partner or in a small group, select one extract you have read. Compare your findings and draw up a flowchart of the writer's argument. On your chart show where the writer uses evidence to back up his or her point of view.

   c On your own, re-read the extract. Then note down any words or phrases that seem to you to push the reader to agree with the writer's point of view.

   d Write a short analysis of the passage, saying what the writer's argument is, how he or she puts it across, and whether or not you find the argument convincing.

3 After reading and studying some or all of the extracts listed on page 179, do the following exercises.

   a Using books, magazines, encyclopaedias and the Internet, research the case for and against animal experiments.

   b Decide your point of view. Then plan your argument, using either a spider diagram or a flowchart.

c Write an essay setting out your point of view on animal experiments – are you for or against it? Use evidence from your research to back up your argument. Make sure your sentences and paragraphs are clearly linked so that the reader can follow what you are saying.

Writing to advise

1 Before you start to read extracts from the above list, complete the following exercises.

a Imagine you are back in Year 6, about to start a new school career in a new school. Draw up a list of ten questions you want answers to about what happens in the new school, what to do and how to behave.

b Note down answers to those ten questions, based on what you now know about life in secondary school.

c Use your notes to write a letter to a Year 6 student, advising him (or her) on what s/he will need to do and know in his (or her) first few weeks at their new school.

2 **a** As you read the extracts from the list on page 181, pay particular attention to the language the writers are using, the kinds of sentences and layout that are used, and how this has all been set out to meet the needs of their expected readership.

   b With a partner or in a small group, select one extract you have all read. Then make notes on this extract under three headings:

   - what advice the writer is giving
   - what the expected readership of the passage may be
   - what examples of vocabulary and sentence structure show the readership being addressed.

   c On your own, write a brief summary of your findings under the three headings above.

3 **a** After reading and studying some or all of the extracts listed on page 181, research the different means of travel, with their costs and the length of the journey, to get from where you live to Madrid in Spain.

   b Write an article for a travel magazine, advising readers on the different ways of getting to Madrid, with their advantages and disadvantages.

Section 4

Writing to analyse, review, comment

If the writers in Section 3 are all writing from a particular point of view or set of beliefs, the writers in this section can be seen as trying to find out what they think about things – some by analysis, as if they are saying, 'What is this about?', others by reviewing their subject, in order to tell their readers whether it is good and in what ways, while the third group of writers is commenting on a topic, as if to say, 'Where does this fit in to what I know already?'

Extract 4.1

This is a review of a CD-Rom based on the children's story *The Little Prince*. What kind of readership do you think Sally Palmer is writing for, and how can you tell?

Tending Roses

The Little Prince
Tivola, £19.99

Whether you read the classic story with original illustrations or watch the beautifully animated version narrated by Kenneth Branagh, this CD-Rom – published to commemorate the 100th anniversary of author Antoine de Saint-Exupery's birth – is sure to delight. 'One only sees clearly with the heart. Anything essential is invisible to the eyes,' says the Little Prince as he leaves Asteroid B-612 to travel the universe, making friends and sharing childlike wisdom as he goes.

There are lots of interactive bits, such as helping the Little Prince to tend his beloved rose; and while accompanying him on his journey, you can click on a fascinating, animated biography of the author, peruse 'planetary log books' or play the curious Fox Taming Game (big patience required here). Oh, and you can even print your own stationery. A great package for fans and newbies alike. ★★★★

Sally Palmer, *Focus*, September 2001

Extract 4.2
Like Extract 4.1, this is a review of a CD-Rom, but this time of a game that teaches an understanding of different scientific processes. As you read it, think about the tone the reviewer uses and the amount of information about the CD-Rom she manages to include in very few words.

Saving the World

Physicus – Save the World with Science!
Tivola, £19.99

This is a good tool for learning about electricity and physical science – and having fun at the same time. The scenario here is that the world has stopped rotating around its own axis, so one half is scorching and the other half is freezing. You have to generate enough electricity so that an enormous repulse from a massive impulse machine kick-starts the planet's rotation again. Physics problems are posed as you locate various energy generators and, to assist you in solving them, you can tap into instructional manuals that, via clear interactive diagrams, teach you how the physical world works. An excellent way to get a good grasp of physics, though ★★★★
PHD holders need not apply.

Sally Palmer, *Focus*, September 2001

Extract 4.3

This passage is a written commentary on a football World Cup qualifier game between old rivals England and Germany. It was published in the *Observer*, a broadsheet newspaper, the day after the game. As you read the article, look at the different kinds of information Paul Wilson is giving the reader – background information, information about what happened in the match and information about what it felt like to be there.

Red Hot England Fire Famous Five

Germany	1
England	5

Paul Wilson at the Olympic Stadium

Uli Hoeness, Franz Beckenbauer and all the other German history men, your team took a hell of a beating. Despite all the pre-match talk Germany have now been beaten twice in World Cup qualifiers and England can proudly claim to have inflicted their heaviest defeat. Michael Owen, with the first hat trick against Germany since 1966 – and with no help from a crossbar or a linesman – did most of it on his own.

When Portugal won in Stuttgart in 1985, there was only one goal in the game and the Germans had already qualified. This victory, which has the added satisfaction of putting England ahead on overall goal difference and leaving the Germans looking at a play-off with Belarus or Ukraine, was as fully deserved as its margin was completely unexpected.

Not even the most brazen optimist expected five goals, especially when Carsten Jancker put the home side ahead after seven minutes. Yet Owen was simply irresistible and he was ably assisted by David Beckham, with Steven Gerrard and Emile Heskey weighing in with a goal each.

It was the home side that mounted the first couple of attacks and England were grateful that Gerrard, as well as Beckham, had passed his fitness test when the Liverpool player's quick reactions foiled a threatening run into the area from Sebastien Deisler.

The Hertha Berlin player had been billed as Germany's danger man and he initiated the opening goal. His chip forward into the penalty area was headed back by Oliver Neuville, catching David Seaman in two minds and to some extent in no man's land. The goalkeeper was powerless to prevent Jancker sweeping the ball home.

England needed to reply quickly and, to the relief of the fans packed behind Oliver Kahn's goal, they were back on level terms within six minutes. Beckham's free-kick from near the left corner flag appeared to have been overhit, but Gerrard diligently chased it down to allow Gary Neville to send it back into the goalmouth from the opposite direction. Nick Barmby gained a priceless flick to wrong foot the German defence and, though the ball came to Owen at an awkward height, he hooked a shot past Kahn for his eighth goal of a season less than a month old.

England were growing in confidence, though the traffic was never entirely one-way. Deisler should have restored Germany's lead after 22 minutes when momentary carelessness by Rio Ferdinand allowed Neuville to pull a cross back from the goal line, but, with the whole of the target to aim for, Deisler shot wide.

Deisler was responsible for an even bigger gaffe on the half-hour when his pass back to Kahn was underhit. With Owen bearing down upon him, the goalkeeper was forced to pick the ball up. With all 11 German players standing on their own goal line England were unable to profit from a free kick from 10 yards out. Beckham's venomous shot hit the wall and Neville's follow-up from the edge of the area sailed over the bar.

Despite a flurry of corners just before half time, the only real German threats came in the time added on for injuries. Jancker set up Bohme for a well-struck, low drive that produced a fantastic, full-length save from Seaman. The importance of that save was fully realised 20 seconds later, when England used the few moments remaining to take a half-time lead.

From Beckham's left-foot cross, Ferdinand nodded the ball back to Gerrard and, from all of 25 yards, he unerringly found the bottom right-hand corner of Kahn's goal with a sweetly struck, low shot.

There was no stopping England now, and although Germany brought on Gerald Asamoah for Marko Rehmer at the start of the second half, he barely had time to touch the ball before his side went another goal down. Again Beckham was the provider, hooking the ball across from the right for Heskey to nod into Owen's path. Kahn got his hand to Owen's shot, but could not keep it out. Somehow, you never doubted that Owen would score.

He was soon celebrating his thirteenth goal for England in 31 games. Running purposefully on to Gerrard's pass, he beat Kahn with a rising shot from just inside the area. England were not finished yet, either. Heskey, played through expertly by Paul Scholes, added a fifth 16 minutes from the end. A few boos rang around the stadium and German spectators started leaving. England supporters have not had so much fun in years.

Paul Wilson, *Observer*, 2nd September 2001

Extract 4.4

This passage from J.R. Ackerley's diary finishes with a twist. It seems to be a straightforward commentary on a small boy's reactions to rabbit hunting, but is it about something else as well?

Rabbiting

Victor and I took little Bernard, aged ten?, for a walk rabbiting. He is the son of an embezzler, serving some years in prison, a curious child with enormous blue eyes, rather uncanny. He begged to be taken. He was dressed in warlike attire – Indian trousers made of sacking, gum boots and a metal rod which he said was a gun. We had not gone far when Tripp, the hotel dog, located a rabbit in a bramble clump and killed it. He took some time to kill it, owing to the thickness of the undergrowth in which they both were, so that he could not get at the rabbit properly. He is said not to be good at killing things anyway. Quick though he is to catch them. So the rabbit squealed and squealed.

The effect on Bernard was most interesting. He almost had hysterics. He was quite overwrought. 'No. No. Oh, look, look. Let me. Let me. There it is. Oh, stop it, stop it' – all that kind of exclamation; he tried to rush into the bush, jumped about, began to cry, pulled himself together, and every now and then looked into my face, gave a sort of smile, and then darted back to the bush again. All within a minute. Victor was very good with him. He commanded him firmly to behave, said he would send him home if he misbehaved, and pulling the still-alive bleeding rabbit out of the bush, dispatched it with a single blow of his hand. Then he told Bernard that he must not be so silly, rabbits were vermin and had to be killed and that if he wanted to come hunting he must get used to it. Bernard recovered and wanted and was allowed to carry the corpse, but every now and then as we walked he remarked, 'I heard it squeal. I heard it squeal.' Later on, since it was awkward from him to carry it by its legs in his hand, we decided to tie my dog's lead to it so that he could sling it over his shoulder. Before doing this, Victor held the rabbit by its ears and shook it, so that the contents of its bowels and bladder fell out. Then he tied my lead round its legs. He pulled the knot tight. 'Not so tight! Not so tight!' cried poor little Bernard, thinking for a moment still that the rabbit was being hurt. Then he appeared to forget and became a mighty hunter, pretending to shoot more rabbits and birds with his metal rod.

Of course it was disgusting, say what one might about vermin, and *I* disliked it too, but life has **inured** me to its horrors. The episode will obviously be remembered all his life. (Though he wanted to come out hunting rabbits, he has always wanted a pet rabbit for his own.) Whether it will affect his life, and if so for good or ill, who can tell. It was certainly a frightful shock to him.

And vermin! How arrogant people are. Does the earth belong to them? Do not the rabbits think *them* vermin too, so to speak. And are they, in fact, not a greater menace to the whole living world than the rabbits themselves?

J.R. Ackerley, from *The Faber Book of Diaries*, ed. Simon Brett

---

inured: hardened

Extract 4.5

The Big Issue is a magazine that is sold on the streets by homeless people to help them earn enough money to get into accommodation and employment. In September 2001 the magazine celebrated its tenth anniversary. This article, published in the anniversary issue, analyses the reasons why it came into being in the first place.

Social Crisis 1991: Why the Big Issue had to happen

During the 1980s, 'The Homeless' became an established part of our society. In the heart of London, along the Strand, in Charing Cross and Lincoln's Inn Fields, hundreds were living on the streets: by night sleeping in tents, on theatre steps, in cardboard boxes and doorways; by day, begging.

Not only were people sleeping rough, but hostels and bed and breakfasts were bulging, and thousands of empty buildings were being squatted. The charity Shelter estimated that in 1991 over half a million people were homeless in England alone.

There are many reasons why people become homeless. Often these individuals carry the baggage of abuse, poor education and lack of motivation. Among them are teenagers coming out of care, people who've left the armed forces, ex-prisoners and people with mental health problems. There are also survivors of broken marriages and relationships, physically abused women, abused young people leaving home, and single parents on low income or benefits.

Under **Thatcher's** governments of the 1980s, local authority new building declined to its lowest peacetime level since 1920. Her administration also

---

Thatcher:　Margaret Thatcher, famous Conservative prime minister had a policy of encouraging home ownership, and giving council tenants the right to buy their homes at lower than market rates. This meant that only undesirable 'sink estates' were left for those housed by local authorities. Meanwhile, the **deregulation** of rents in the **private sector** brought soaring rents: a severe shortage of affordable accommodation became the norm. Then, at the end of the 1980s soaring interest rates affected mortgages, resulting in arrears, repossessions and negative equity for many.

At the same time, changes to the social security structure eroded benefits for the homeless, and for young people in particular. 16 and 17-year-olds lost entitlement to income support from September 1988. These changes, combined with an unemployment crisis in the North around the same time, saw increasing numbers of poverty-stricken people migrating to London.

David Warner worked for the charity Homeless Network. He says: 'a lot of different things came together in the early eighties that led to the massive explosion of people on the streets.

'Firstly, there was the closure programme of old DHS spikes [hostels for single people], starting around 1981/82.' The government was replacing these inhumane places with a more diverse range of accommodation, mainly through housing associations.

At the same time, there were very large working men's hostels, privately owned, which had increasingly become dumping grounds for people considered 'social misfits'. Making these places fit to live in meant reducing numbers of bed spaces, a measure that impacted across London particularly, but also elsewhere.

---

deregulation: removal of regulations
private sector: with private landlords rather than local council or housing association housing

Homeless people didn't like these big hostels. 'I've been in Salvation Army hostels,' says Jim Lawrie. 'Their attitude in the past has been "it's really your fault, but God loves you." They used to go and recruit the sinner. I was in one 20 years ago in Middlesex Street. It was dormitory accommodation and you used to have to sleep with your boots under your bed, or someone would nick them in the middle of the night. Things have moved on since then, with more modern hostels. Some of the attitude is the same. I make a point of not going into their hostels, or not going into hostels at all.'

Nick Hardwick, then Director of Centrepoint which works with young homeless people, emphasises that, in the 1980s, kids weren't called 'homeless', they were 'runaways' – a term that implied that they could be counselled and sent back home. He recalls: 'the idea that people didn't have homes was not an argument that had been completely won. Homelessness was seen as a social condition, something about the way you behave, rather than you not having anywhere to live.'

Victor Adebowale, CEO of Centrepoint, puts the blame squarely on the government of the time. He says: 'Most of the Tory party didn't care or know about the consequences. Their thinking was, "if it works for the majority, hell, we can live with a few homeless people."'

The Big Issue, 3–9 September 2001

Extract 4.6
Stephen Clift has made a study of the ways in which different magazines deal with the topic of holiday romances. Here he looks at how the topic is presented in one magazine for young teenage girls.

Romance and Sex on Holidays Abroad

The 'Holiday Special' edition of *My Guy Magazine* contains a variety of 'sensational' photo-stories and features which have a bearing on the theme of holiday relationships and 'romance'. The magazine appears to be aimed at a mid to late teenage market, although the letters section, revealingly entitled 'One from the heart . . .', includes two letters from 13 year-olds. The very term 'romance' serves to encapsulate the concerns with relationship and emotional issues which characterise much of the literature available to girls and young women from an early age. Magazines exploring such issues are not marketed towards boys and young men of a similar age group, and as we shall see, by the time the topic of holidays appears in 'men's' magazines, the concern is almost exclusively with the stereotypically macho one of 'scoring' with little or no attention given to relationship or emotional issues.

In one of the photo-stories 'Getting away from it', 'Anna had come on holiday to forget'. Her boyfriend, we learn during the story, had walked out on her and her whole life had fallen apart and now she is on holiday alone 'to try and forget'. The basic storyline involves her meeting a young man who claims to be German, by the name of Rolf. He is clearly interested in her but she doesn't want to get involved. They have a glass of coke together and she explains her situation and Rolf assures her 'I am not interested in your heart'. They play a game of giant chess, the game is a success and Rolf wants to meet again the following day. Anna is uncertain, but Rolf again reassures her, in a form of broken English which even the least linguistically competent German in unlikely to use: 'Remember, you cannot in love with me be falling. We live in different countries.' The next day, Rolf persists in following her, an argument ensues and Anna accidentally pushes him over a railing and he falls some distance on to the beach. Anna is horrified, rushes to help him, and, as she cradles him in her arms . . . 'He reached up and kissed her with soft, but forceful lips.'

'From then on they were inseparable.' They see the sights together, swim and bathe together and all too soon their last evening together arrives. Now she admits that she's feeling sad because she's leaving him: 'I know I vowed not to' she tells him 'But I've fallen head over heels in love with you.' Rolf tells her 'That's the luck of the draw' and at this point the penny drops as Anna realises that 'the luck of the draw' is not a German phrase! So Rolf finally admits to being English and rather shame-facedly apologizes. Anna's reaction is one of delight: 'But don't you see, this is perfect, absolutely perfect! Because now we can be together. You'll be coming back to England and we can stay in touch!' But it's not to be. Although Rolf is English, he does live in Germany and Anna responds: 'I see. So I'll probably never see you again.' Rolf's reply, 'Probably not. I'm sorry. I guess it just wasn't meant to be . . .' brings the sorry moral tale to its rather feeble conclusion.

Clearly, any young woman on holiday needs to be wary of the 'Rolfs' of this world who pretend to be something they are not and who blatantly take advantage of a girl they know to be vulnerable. The message of this story is further reinforced in a guide to the 'Boys of Summer' which comes later.

The reader is warned about such types as: 'The Fun-Lover' – just 'one of ver lads' who will 'spend all day dive-bombing the bits of the pool you're swimming in'; 'The Single Poseur' – 'drop-dead gorge!' but 'so full of himself he'll hardly notice you' and 'The Action Man' – 'He'll be too busy bungee-jumping off a bridge or running through the dunes' so 'If you do manage to get close, he'll be so sweaty anyway that you'll need to back off!' What every girl really wants is 'The Old Romantic' – 'He'll give you flowers and 'I love U' cards and deck you out in coral jewellery to make you feel special.'

But 'romance' on holiday is a serious matter and to underline this point, the issue includes a full page listing '10 things to avoid on holiday'. On the one hand, the reader is advised not to take things too seriously and develop unrealistic expectations:

> DON'T think that a holiday romance will last. You don't have to stay away from boys full-stop to avoid getting hurt, but keep things casual and not too heavy. Remember . . . 90% of holiday romances don't last more than two weeks!

But on the other hand, she is cautioned against being too casual:

> DON'T rush into having sex with someone just because you're on holiday! It may seem like paradise to be surrounded by sea, sand and sea, but try to avoid sleeping with the nearest male just for the sake of it.

The injunction not to 'rush into having sex' is the only direct reference to sex in the entire magazine. The tone is clearly negative and highlights the contradictoriness and difficulty of the young woman's position: don't get too serious but don't be too casual. Whatever option is taken, the striking thing is that no references are made to sexual health risks nor to the need to practise safer sex. The idea that a girl might simply enjoy having sex without emotional involvement and yet would be responsible about protecting her sexual health and avoiding unwanted pregnancy appears to have no place within *My Guy*'s conceptual framework.

Finally, after the fiction, the humour and the direct advice, come the true confessions: 'Holiday Romances. Do They Ever Last?', 'We talked to two girls who have very different stories to tell . . . '. In the first, Louise describes meeting Tim while on holiday with her parents in Portugal. Louise was clearly much more interested in Tim than he was in her and 'By the end of the second week I'd really fallen for him.' However, by this time they 'had only kissed twice, little kisses, not properly' and Louise 'was convinced it was because Tim respected me and wanted to wait until we got home before we got into anything more serious.' So, not surprisingly, Louise was shocked when Tim told her he didn't think it was 'worth it' to keep in touch:

> Turns out he'd really enjoyed my company, and he thought my mum and dad were brilliant, but he only liked me as a friend. I wasn't his type. Simple really. At least he didn't promise to phone and then just not bother to . . .

Reflecting on the experience later, Louise feels she 'should have realised' that she and her parents were just someone at the hotel for Tim to 'latch on to' – and interestingly, she concludes by saying: 'My holidays now consist of sun and fun – boys are out!' In other words, having made the mistake of taking things too seriously with Tim, the only course of action open to her in future is to avoid boys – the options appear to be 'a serious relationship' or nothing.

Stephen Clift, *Romance and Sex on Holidays Abroad: a study of magazine representations*

Extract 4.7

In this article from *The Ecologist* magazine, Sonia Shah comments on the fact that there are more tigers kept as pets in America than there are tigers left in the wild. What do you think her attitude is to those who keep tigers as pets? Is it straightforward?

Where Have All the Tigers Gone?

There are more pet tigers in America than wild tigers in the rest of the world. What on earth is going on?

Everyone knows that the tiger is one of the world's endangered species. With the panda, whale and elephant, it's one of the media's favourite 'struggling wildlife' icons. Yet, bizarrely, while its numbers are slipping in its natural Asian habitats, a new kind of tiger is doing rather well over in America. The pet tiger.

According to the Zoological Society of London, between 5,000 and 7,000 tigers live in the wild around the world. Yet at least as many pace in cages owned by private American citizens, who own between 6,000 and 7,000 endangered tigers as pets, according to the US-based Animal Protection Institute.

While the 1973 US Endangered Species Act and the 1975 international Convention on International Trade in Endangered Species of Wild Flora and Fauna cracked down on the taking of endangered animals from the wild, neither act regulates what happens to the **progeny** of the endangered animals brought to the United States before their passage. Today, owning a captive-born endangered animal is legal in 31 US states. Breeding and selling these animals requires a

progeny: offspring

few permits and licences, which even some endangered-cat owners say are too easy to obtain.

Much of the private trade in endangered tigers originated in 'surplus' tigers dumped by zoos. Zoos hungry for the outpouring of public attention paid to new zoo babies bred more tigers than they could keep, and ended up selling the surplus cubs to private breeders, who in turn sold the animals to auctioneers, hunting farms, and pet-owners. US-based trade magazines such as *Animal Marketplace Magazine* and *Animal Finder's Guide* list exotic animal sales and auctions, along with ads from tiger breeders and pet owners, **soliciting** purchases ($3,500 for a pair of Bengal tigers), trades (12-week-old de-clawed Siberian tiger for baby lynx or cougar), and 'jungle-cat reduction sales'. There are dozens of internet sites and even private associations such as the National Alternative Pet Association that promote private ownership of exotic and endangered species.

But why should a private American citizen want to own a huge, **carnivorous** Asian predator? 'Something about their sleek bodies, graceful movements, self-assured independence, and raw power,' wrote one big-cat owner, 'attracts like no other animal.' This intoxicating attraction is almost sexual: 'you can almost feel the smooth ripple of rock hard muscles as the cat shifts slightly to put its massive head in your lap. The rumble as the cat begins to purr is so deep it is felt more than heard, and echoes through your body until your whole being resonates with its subdued power.'

Once they own an exotic animal, many eventually turn into self-made conservationists, incorporating

---

soliciting: seeking, asking for
carnivorous: meat-eating

their farms and ranches as non-profit nature centres. Although some may be managed well, others are clearly politically correct cover for poorly executed exotic-pet-ownership. The Tigers Only Preserve in New Jersey traces its founding to 1976, when a former circus employee bought two Bengal tiger cubs from a big-cat trainer at a New Jersey theme park. She kept them in a barn next to her rented apartment. In 1987, Joan Byron-Marasek's permit was denied because of the inadequacy of her facilities. Three of the tiger sub-species she wanted covered by the permit were already extinct, which gives a sense of her knowledge of the endangered tigers she professed to want to save.

But the next year her permit came through and, by 1999, she had over two dozen tigers on her 12-acre compound in New Jersey, which is closed to the public. Over a decade of annual inspections had

apparently found little amiss, yet in January 1999, one of her tigers escaped the compound and wandered the New Jersey suburbs for seven hours before being shot and killed by state officials.

The incident threw a rare light on the preserve, which few neighbours knew about. A curator from the Bronx Zoo who was brought in to inspect it called the preserve the 'worst facility that I have ever seen', citing rotting deer carcasses, cramped facilities, rat infestations, and evidence of malnourishment among the tigers. While neighbours hustled together a lawsuit against her and state authorities attempted to shut her preserve down, Byron-Marasek went on breeding her tigers, and five more were born in April 1999. The state wildlife agency issued her a permit to use the tigers for advertising and other theatrical purposes, but authorities found no evidence of either.

Apart from canned-hunt ranches, where, for a few thousand dollars, hunters can shoot an endangered cat at close range, Americans who own tigers – whether as livestock, pets, or rescued victims – all claim that they are saving this endangered species from extinction. 'I like raising animals that are rare or endangered,' says *Animal Finder's Guide* founder Pat Hoctor. 'Since there is less land each day available to animals due to man's **encroachment**, I feel animals must exist in captivity or face extinction.' Yet according to zoologists, most of the thousands of privately owned tigers in the United States, as well as close to 200 of all zoo tigers, are hybridised, 'generic' or 'mutt' tigers. Breeders introduced jungle-dwelling tigers to Siberian tigers, to produce these generic tigers that could never survive in the wild.

---

encroachment: invasion, taking over territory

The scientific breeding programme that accredited zoos around the world introduced to their tigers in the 1980s, while **laudable**, may not help save tigers either. These zoos have weeded out generic tigers and instead bred captive tigers to maintain sub-species lines. The idea is to create a 'genetic reservoir' that could be re-introduced into the wild or used to re-seed a new wild population.

Scientists have introduced other captive-born endangered species into the wild, in expensive, time-consuming and small-scale projects that have shown mixed results to date. But for zoo tigers, this unlocking of the doors seems especially unlikely, zoo officials say. The wilderness to introduce them to shrinks daily. Regionally, the human poverty, maldevelopment, and pollution that threaten wild tigers show no signs of **abating**. Until the world solves these colossal, global problems, there's little chance for any tigers in the wild, captive-born or not.

So why do American zoos keep tigers at all? Zoos claim that their tiger exhibits play a crucial educational role, alerting the 300 million people who visit the world's zoos to the problems facing endangered species. Clearly, American zoo exhibits have inspired a deep love for these majestic creatures that normally live so very far away. The Tiger Information Centre at the Minnesota Zoo receives volumes of mail from people who write, 'I love tigers. How can I buy one?'

The desire to possess a creature doesn't appear to **mitigate** pet-tiger-owners' desire to save them as well. For them, conservation is ultimately about providing a

---

laudable: praise-worthy
abating: reducing, going down
mitigate: reduce

safe and loving home to a seemingly homeless endangered animal. According to this brand of conservation ethics, all a tiger really needs is a healthy dose of human love. And love the animals they do. Many cherish their tigers even after (or perhaps because of) evidence of their anti-human ferocity. One pet tiger bit the head of his owner, ripping his jaw and ear canal out of his skull. The recovered owner still owns two Bengal tiger cubs and four adult tigers. He said the mauling 'hasn't changed the way I look at them'. Another woman let her daughter sleep with a tiger cub, which later severed the 10-year-old girl's **carotid artery** and killed her.

These adored tigers and their adoring owners may symbolise the final conquest of a novel kind of ecological imperialism. The living, roaring animal, 'its repertory stunted by the impoverished constraints of human care,' as biologist E.O. Wilson put it, is subdued in its cage as an unlikely plaything, 'a mute speaker trapped inside the unnatural clearing, like a messenger to me from an unexplored world'.

But pet-tiger-owners' passion for the animals is real. 'I feel it's my mission to save these animals from extinction,' Joan Byron-Marasek says. 'I know I'm doing it better than any other place.'

Sonia Shah, *The Ecologist*, vol 31 no 7, September 2001

---

carotid artery: the main supply of blood to the head and neck

Extract 4.8
Oliver Sacks is a well-known neuro-biologist, working particularly on the connection between the ways in which our brains work and how we see ourselves and are able to function as people. When he went abroad on a walking holiday and had a bad fall down a mountainside, which landed him in hospital, he became his own subject of study as he tracked his relationship with reality through the different stages of injury and recovery. Here he has just been flown home to have an operation on his damaged leg.

Becoming a Patient

As I was taken in the ambulance from London airport, to the great hospital where I was to be operated on the next day, my good humour and sanity began to leave me, and in their place came a most terrible dread. I cannot call it the dread of death, though doubtless that was contained in it. It was rather a dread of something dark and nameless and secret – a nightmarish feeling, uncanny and ominous, such as I had not experienced on the Mountain at all. Then, on the whole, I had faced what reality had in store, but now I felt distortion rising, taking over. I saw it, I felt it, and I felt powerless to combat it. It would not go away, and the most I could do was sit tight and hold fast, murmuring a **litany** of commonsense and reassurance to myself. The journey in the ambulance was a bad trip, in all ways – and behind the dread (which I could not vanquish as its creator), I felt delirium rocking my mind – such a delirium as I had used to know, all too well, as a child,

---

litany: series of prayers

wherever I was feverish or had one of my migraines. My brother, who was riding with me, observed some of this, and said:

'Easy now, Ollie, it won't be so bad. But you *do* look dead white, and clammy and ill. I think you've a fever and you look toxic and shocked. Try and rest. Keep calm. Nothing terrible will happen.'

Yes, indeed I had a fever. I felt myself burning and freezing. Obsessive fears gnawed at my mind. My perceptions were unstable. Things seemed to change – to lose their reality and become, in **Rilke**'s phrase, 'things made of fear'. The hospital, a prosaic Victorian building, looked for a moment like the Tower of London. The wheeled stretcher I was placed on made me think of a **tumbril**, and the tiny room I was given, with its window blocked out (it had been improvised at the last minute, all the wards and side wards being taken), put me in mind of the notorious torture chamber, 'Little Ease', in the Tower. Later, I was to become very fond of my tiny womb-like room . . . But on that ghastly, ominous evening of the 25th, seized by fever and fantastical neurosis, shaking with secret dread, I perceived everything amiss and could do nothing about it.

'Execution tomorrow,' said the clerk in Admissions.

I knew it must have been '*Operation* tomorrow', but the feeling of execution overwhelmed what he said. And if my room was 'Little Ease', it was also the Condemned Cell. I could see in my mind with hallucinatory vividness, the famous engraving of **Fagin** in his cell. My gallows – humour consoled me and undid me and got me through the other grotesqueries of admission. (It was only up on

---

Rilke: Rainer Maria Rilke, famous German poet
tumbril: the type of cart on which people were taken to be executed during the French Revolution
Fagin: famous villain from Charles Dickens' novel *Oliver Twist*

the ward that humanity broke in.) And to these grotesque fantasies were added the realities of admission, the systematic depersonalisation which goes with becoming-a-patient. One's own clothes are replaced by an anonymous white nightgown, one's wrist is clasped by an identification bracelet with a number. One becomes subject to institutional rules and regulations. One is no longer a free agent; one no longer has rights; one is no longer in the world-at-large. It is strictly **analogous to** becoming a prisoner, and humiliatingly reminiscent of one's first day at school. One is no longer a person – one is now an inmate. One understands that this is protective, but it is quite dreadful too. And I was seized, overwhelmed, by this dread, this elemental sense and dread of degradation, throughout the dragged-out formalities of admission until – suddenly, wonderfully – humanity broke in, in the first lovely moment I was addressed as myself, and not merely as an admission, a *thing*.

Suddenly into my condemned cell a nice jolly Staff-Nurse, with a Lancashire accent, burst in, a person, a woman, sympathetic – and comic. She was 'tickled pink', as she put it, when she unpacked my rucksack and found fifty books and a virtual absence of clothes.

'Oh, Dr Sacks, you're potty!' she said, and burst into jolly laughter.

And then I laughed too. And in that healthy laughter the tension broke and the devils disappeared.

Oliver Sacks, *A Leg to Stand On*

---

analogous to: like, comparable to

Extract 4.9

In a book called *Learning to Labour*, Paul Willis looks at the way some young people find school irrelevant to the way in which they live their lives. Here he interviews some teenage boys who have developed not doing schoolwork into a fine art and analyses his findings.

Dossing, Blagging and Wagging

Opposition to school is **principally manifested** in the struggle to win symbolic and physical space from the institution and its rules and to defeat its main perceived purpose: to make you 'work'. Both the winning and the prize – a form of self-direction – profoundly develop informal cultural meanings and practices. The dynamic aspect of the staff/pupil relationship will be examined later on. By the time a counter-school culture is fully developed its members have become adept at managing the formal system, and limiting its demands to the absolute minimum. Exploiting the complexity of modern regimes of mixed ability groupings, blocked timetabling and multiple options, in many cases this minimum is simply the act of registration.

[In a group discussion on the school curriculum]

Joey   . . . of a Monday afternoon, we'd have nothing right? Nothing hardly relating to school work, Tuesday afternoon we have swimming and they stick you in a classroom for the rest of the afternoon, Wednesday afternoon you have games and there's only Thursday and Friday

---

principally manifested: mainly shown

afternoon that you work, if you call that work. The last lesson Friday afternoon we used to go and doss, half of us wagged out o' lessons and the other half go to the classroom, sit down and just go to sleep . . .

Spansky . . . Skive this lesson, go up on the bank, have a smoke, and the next lesson who, you know, 'll call the register . . .

Bill   It's easy to go home as well, like him [Eddie] . . . last Wednesday afternoon, he got his mark and went home . . .

Eddie   I ain't supposed to be in school this afternoon, I'm supposed to be at college [in a link course where students spend one day a week at college for vocational instruction].

* * *

PW   What's the last time you've done some writing?
Will   When we done some writing?
Fuzz   Oh are, last time was in careers, 'cos I writ 'yes' on a piece of paper, that broke me heart.
PW   Why did it break your heart?
Fuzz   I mean to write, 'cos I was going to try and go through the term without writing anything. 'Cos since we've cum back, I ain't done nothing [it was half way through term].

Truancy is a very imprecise – even meaningless – measure of rejection of school. This is not only because of the practice of stopping in school for registration before 'wagging off' (developed to a fine art amongst 'the lads'), but also because it only measures one aspect of what we might most accurately describe as informal student **mobility**. Some of 'the lads' develop the ability of moving

---

mobility: movement, ability to move

about the school at their own will to a remarkable degree. They construct virtually their own day from what is offered by the school. Truancy is one relatively unimportant and crude variant of this principle of self-direction which ranges across vast chunks of the syllabus and covers many **diverse** activities: being free out of class, being in class and doing no work, being in the wrong class, roaming the corridors looking for excitement, being asleep in private. The core skill which articulates these possibilities is being able to get out of any given class: the preservation of personal mobility.

[In a group discussion]

PW But doesn't anybody worry about you not being in their class?

Fuzz I get a note off the cooks saying I'm helping them …

John You just go to him [a teacher] and say, 'Can I go and do a job.' He'll say, 'Certainly, by all means', 'cos they want to get rid of you like.

Fuzz Specially when I ask 'em.

* * *

Pete You know the holes in the corridor, I didn't want to go to games, he told me to fetch his keys, so I dropped them down the hole in the corridor, and had to go and get a torch and find them.

For the successful, there can be an embarrassment of riches. It can become difficult to choose between self-organised routes through the day.

Will . . . what we been doing, playing cards in this room 'cos we can lock the door.

---

diverse: different

PW Which room's this now?

Will Resources centre, where we're making the frames [a new stage for the deputy head], s'posed to be.

PW Oh! You're still making the frames!

Will We should have had it finished, we just lie there on top of the frames, playing cards, or trying to get to sleep . . . Well, it gets a bit boring, I'd rather go and sit in the classroom, you know.

PW What sort of lessons would you think of going into?

Will Uh, science, I think, 'cos you can have a laff in there sometimes.

This self-direction and thwarting of formal organisational aims is also an assault on official notions of time. The most arduous task of the deputy head is the construction of the timetables. In large schools, with several options open to the fifth year [Year 10], everything has to be fitted in with the greatest care. The first weeks of term are spent in continuous revision, as junior members of staff complain, and particular combinations are shown to be unworkable. Time, like money, is valuable and not to be squandered. Everything has to be ordered into a kind of massive critical path of the school's purpose. Subjects become measured blocks of time in careful relation to each other ... The complex charts on the deputy head's wall show how it works. In theory it is possible to check where every individual is at every moment of the day. But for 'the lads' this never seems to work. If one wishes to contact them, it is much more important to know and understand their own rhythms and patterns of movement. These rhythms reject the obvious purposes of the timetable and their implicit notions of time. The common complaint about 'the lads' from staff and 'ear-'oles' is that they 'waste valuable time'. Time for 'the lads' is not something you carefully husband and thoughtfully spend on the achievement of desired objectives in the future. For 'the lads' time is something they want to claim for themselves now, as an aspect of their immediate identity and self-direction. Time is used for the preservation of a state – being with 'the lads' – not for the achievement of a goal – qualifications.

Paul Willis, *Learning to Labour*

Extract 4.10
This passage comes from a book published in 1877. It was written for Victorian children to give them some idea of what it would have been like to have been a child in the previous century – and now we are reading it over a hundred years later . . . In this extract, Sarah Tytler comments on the home life of middle-class children brought up in the country.

Children of the Middle Class

Boys and girls who had not the honour to be lords and ladies, of course fared harder in one sense, and had **homelier** duties. Very soon, if the family were a large one, and its purse not too full, the young people were made useful. The little girl saved her mother an additional servant; the little boy was proud to act, when in the house, as page, porter, family message-boy, and that with no loss of consideration from their equals.

If the family lived in town, the children went, as I have said to the nearest school. If the household happened to be established in the country – far from a school it might be – the busy, **cumbered** mother somehow contrived to teach the children to read, and often also to write and **cipher**. If their education went farther, some assistance was called in, in the shape of a tutor or a governess for six months or a year. In other cases the father, if he were a clergyman, and receiving other pupils, generally supplied the finishing touches, instructing the boy in

homelier: more ordinary
cumbered: overwhelmed, overburdened
to cipher: to do arithmetic, to count

Latin and Greek, to fit him for **taking orders** in his turn, or rubbing up the daughter's French or Italian in order to give Jenny or Prue an advantage which she might turn to account in earning a livelihood, supposing she lost her father before she found a husband.

If the boys were not destined for a profession, they were early launched in their other callings, and were sent in waggons or they trudged on foot fifteen or twenty miles to their destinations to do for themselves. The outfit of **stout wearing apparel** with which the mother carefully packed their trunks, and the little dainties which the motherly heart stowed away in its recesses, were often the parents' last contribution to the lads' maintenance. With regard to these treats, which were intended to soften the pain of parting and the loneliness of beginning life among strangers, there is a pretty story told of the great and good Lord Collingwood. When he started to join his first ship as a midshipman, his mother had placed a plum-cake in his box. The affectionate little fellow was overwhelmed with grief of the leave-taking, and the strangeness of the new world in which he found himself, and where he had not yet a recognised place or a duty to perform. He sat down disconsolately on deck. A kind-hearted lieutenant came up and spoke cheerily to the youngster. Responding warmly and gratefully, as he ever did to the least friendliness, the boy requested his new acquaintance to come down with him to the cockpit; there, opening his box, little Collingwood pressed on his grown-up friend the best he had to give, a large slice of the plum-cake, which was to have been his own consolation.

Where the boy, after his lesson hours, made himself generally useful – whether by **making the markets** (if he

---

taking orders: becoming a clergyman
stout wearing apparel: strong clothes
making the markets: doing the shopping

happened to be specially trustworthy) and being his father's **runner**, or by digging and weeding the garden, and helping to groom the horse and fodder the cow – the girl dressed and nursed the young children, and entered on an extensive department of her education, and which was regarded as much more serious and **incumbent** than book-learning.

She started **betimes** to become a thorough mistress of the whole economy of a household, and to aspire to be as good as a professional – not a mere amateur or fancy – sempstress or cook. When her mother was laid aside by illness, or on rare occasions when she went from home – possibly to attend the death-bed of her aged father or mother, whom she had not seen since she left them – **hale** middle-aged people, in the old home which she had quitted as a bride; or, happily, on a joyful instead of a mournful errand, to be present at a favourite brother or sister's wedding – the whole burden of the housekeeping devolved on the little maid, deputy and substitute. She stood gallantly at her post, though well-nigh crushed by the amount of her responsibility, and by the number and variety of the counsels and warnings which were administered to her. Her brother, though he was her support and protector out of doors, was, as all girls will know, little good in the house. Nay, she had to see that he did not shirk cleaning himself, and making himself look like a professional man's son when his work was done, or that he did not forget to change his clothes when he came in wet from a duck in the river.

If the establishment were in the country, and the season were summer – as indeed remote visiting was

---

runner: messenger
incumbent: necessary, a duty
betimes: early
hale: healthy

hardly to be thought of at any other season – the young housekeeper had also the dairy, the poultry, the summer bleaching of linen, and such preserving and pickling as belonged to the month, on her mind. It might be that Molly in the kitchen was getting old, and had to trust much to an ignorant, stupid girl from the village, serving her apprenticeship in the vicar's kitchen. But the little mistress had a very fair notion of how much milk Cowslip ought to give, and how much butter each churning should yield, since she had skimmed the cream off the basins for the last year, and she had done the better part of the churning when Molly was busy with the great wash. She knew all the cocks, hens, and chickens, and every goose and duck – indeed they were her particular friends; yet it was an arduous task to have to account for all the eggs which the mothers of the tribes ought to have layed, **to 'set' the hens**, and to be answerable for their good behaviour during the period of sitting, besides looking after every fluffy little bird which issued from an egg. These pretty black and white and speckled chickens, yellow and brown ducklings, and grey goslings, were at once the delight and the torment of our small friend's reign. She was very fond of them, still it was hard that silly old hens would wander away with their families from comfortable hen-coops, and lose themselves among wet corn; and vagrant ducks, that might have been content in their own nice pond, would **levant** with their offspring to join their wild brethren in the trout stream. And their aggrieved mistress had no sooner engaged in any difficult and important task, such as salting the green walnuts, than she was sharply summoned – frequently on false alarms – by sundry chirpings, cluckings, and quackings, to fling everything

---

to 'set' the hens: to put the hens on their nests to hatch their eggs
levant: wander off

down and run into the yard, lest a hawk should be in the air, or a fox stealing round the corner . . .

The little girl could not have done a **tithe** of it all if she had not been well accustomed to the details – if she had served as her mother's right hand when the mistress was at home, almost since the daughter could remember anything. Certainly she had darned all her father's stockings when she was eight, and made him a shirt before she was twelve years of age.

For the middle-class girl took plain work as her portion. She rested her aspirations on attaining the height of skill and diligence which should enable her to make a shirt – the felling, stitching, and button-holing of which should be complete and unexceptionable – in the course of one long summer day; or in mixing and putting together an apple dumpling, which should be as hard as a cannon ball to the touch, and as light as a feather to the digestion. To assist to make her frocks or to throw off a tea-cake was her fancy work, if the former could be considered fancy-work, when grave interests depended upon it. It was one of the youthful frock-maker's cherished projects, if she should not marry like her mother, and if anything happened to father, rather than be parted from all she loved, by going out and knocking about the world as a governess, to take advantage of her early practice, and of the three months at dressmaking which she had been promised when she grew up, to become a full-fledged dressmaker in her own person, and provide a home for mother and the children.

Sarah Tytler, *Childhood a Hundred Years Ago*

---

tithe: one-tenth

Extract 4.11

William Gibson is a novelist who sets his stories in some fictional future world. In this article he comments on present-day Japan, and how, to him, it represents the way in which the future will develop.

My Own Private Tokyo

I wish I had a thousand-yen note for every journalist who, over the past decade, has asked me whether Japan is still as futurologically sexy as it seemed to be in the '80s. If I did, I'd take one of these spotlessly lace-upholstered taxis over to **the Ginza** and buy my wife a small box of the most expensive Belgian chocolates in the universe.

I'm back to Tokyo tonight to refresh my sense of place, check out the **post-Bubble city**, professionally resharpen that handy Japanese edge. If you believe, as I do, that all cultural change is essentially technology-driven, you pay attention to Japan. There are reasons for that, and they run deep.

Dining late, in a plastic-draped gypsy noodle stall in Shinjuku, the classic cliché better-than-*Blade Runner* Tokyo street set, I scope my neighbour's phone as he checks his text messages. Wafer-thin, Kandy Kolor pearlescent white, complexly curvilinear, totally **ephemeral** looking, its screen seethes with a miniature version of **Shinjuku's** neon light show. He's got the **rosary**-like **anticancer** charm attached; most people

---

the Ginza: the main shopping area of Tokyo
post-Bubble city: built following the great economic expansion of the 1980s
ephemeral: fragile, short-lived, not long-lasting
Shinjuku: entertainment district of Tokyo
rosary: a string of beads used for counting through a set of prayers
anticancer: against the cancer thought to be caused by radiation from portable phones

here do, believing it deflects microwaves, grounding them away from the brain. It looks great, in terms of a novelist's need for props, but it actually may not be that next-generation in terms of what I'm used to back home.

Tokyo has been my handiest prop shop for as long as I've been writing: sheer eye candy. You can see more chronological strata of futuristic design in a Tokyo streetscape than anywhere else in the world. Like successive layers of Tomorrowlands, older ones showing through when the newer ones start to peel.

So the pearlescent phone with the cancer thingy gets drafted straight into props, but what about Japan itself? The Bubble's gone, successive economic plans sputter and wobble to the same halt, one political scandal follows another ... Is that the future?

Yes. Part of it, and not necessarily ours, but definitely yes. The Japanese love 'futuristic' things precisely because they've been living in the future for such a very long time now. History, that other form of speculative fiction, explains why.

The Japanese, you see, have been repeatedly dropkicked ever further down the time-line, by serial national traumata of quite unthinkable weirdness, by 150 years of deep, almost constant, change. The 20th century, for Japan, was like a ride on a rocket sled, with successive bundles of fuel igniting spontaneously, one after another.

They have had one strange ride, the Japanese, and we tend to forget that.

In 1854, with **Commodore Perry's** second landing, **gunboat diplomacy** ended 200 years of self-imposed isolation, a deliberate stretching out of the feudal dreamtime. The Japanese knew that America, not to

---

Commodore Perry: American naval commander
gunboat diplomacy: enforcing your national interests through the threat of armed attack

be denied, had come knocking with the future in its hip pocket. This was the **quintessential cargo-cult** moment for Japan: the arrival of alien tech.

The people who ran Japan – the emperor, the lords and ladies of his court, the nobles, and the very wealthy – were entranced. It must have seemed as though these visitors emerged from some rip in the fabric of reality. Imagine the **Roswell Incident** as a trade mission, a successful one: imagine us buying all the **Gray technology** we could afford, no reverse engineering required. This was a cargo cult where the cargo actually did what it claimed to do.

They must all have gone briefly but thoroughly mad, then pulled it together somehow and plunged on. The Industrial Revolution came whole, in kit form: steamships, railroads, telegraphy, factories, Western medicine, the division of labour – not to mention a mechanized military and the political will to use it. Then those Americans returned to whack Asia's first industrial society **with the light of a thousand suns** – twice, and very hard – and thus the War ended.

At which point the aliens arrived in force, this time with briefcases and plans, bent on a cultural retrofit from the scorched earth up. Certain central aspects of the feudal-industrial core were left intact, while other areas

---

quintessential: purest

cargo-cult: a religion that sprang up in New Guinea after the arrival of Europeans, in which they believed that the ghosts of their ancestors would arrive bringing them food, tobacco, axes and other goods

Roswell Incident: when aliens, called Grays, are supposed to have crash-landed near Roswell in the United States

Gray technology: alien technology

the light of a thousand suns: nuclear explosions caused by the atomic bombs dropped on Hiroshima and Nagasaki

of the nation's political and business culture were heavily grafted with American tissue, resulting in **hybrid** forms.

And tonight, watching the Japanese do what they do here, amid all this electric **kitsch**, all this randomly overlapped media, this chaotically stable neon storm of marketing hoopla, I've got my answer: Japan is still the future, and if the vertigo is gone, it really only means that they've made it out the far end of that tunnel of prematurely accelerated change. Here, in the first city to have this firmly and this comfortably arrived in this new century – the most truly contemporary city on earth – **the centre is holding**.

In a world of technologically driven **exponential** change, the Japanese have an acquired edge: they know how to live with it. Nobody legislates that kind of change into being, it just comes, and keeps coming, and the Japanese have been experiencing it for more than a hundred years.

I see them poised here tonight, hanging out, life going on, in the glow of these very big televisions. Postgraduates of all this.

Home at last, in the 21st century.

William Gibson, *Wired*, September 2001

---

hybrid: cross-bred, mongrel
kitsch: tasteless but popular art
the centre is holding: a reference to a poem by the Irish poet
W.B. Yeats, in which he sees everything falling to pieces: 'the centre cannot hold / Mere anarchy is loosed upon the world'
exponential: rapidly increasing

Extract 4.12

This short extract is from a book that looks at the way in which historians and journalists have discussed America's use of atomic weapons over Japan in the last days of the Second World War. At different times there have been different attitudes to and an emphasis on different aspects of the decision to use the bombs and on the effects of their use. Here the writer analyses our current understanding of how and why the bombs came to be used.

The Decision to Use the Bomb

Careful scholarly treatment of the records and manuscripts opened over the past few years has greatly **enhanced** our understanding of why the **Truman** administration used atomic weapons against Japan. Experts continue to disagree on some issues, but critical questions have been answered. The consensus among scholars is that the bomb was not needed to avoid an invasion of Japan and to end the war within a relatively short time. It is clear that alternatives to the bomb existed and that Truman and his advisers knew it. Furthermore, most scholars, at least **in retrospect**, regard an invasion as a remote possibility. Whether the bomb shortened the war and saved lives among those fighting in the Pacific is much more difficult to ascertain. Some analysts have argued that the war would have ended just as soon, or even sooner, if American leaders had pursued available

---

enhanced: improved
Truman: Harry S. Truman, President of the United States at the end of the Second World War
in retrospect: looking back

alternatives, but this is speculative and a matter of continuing debate. It is certain that the **hoary** claim that the bomb prevented half a million or more American combat deaths cannot be supported by the available evidence. The issue of whether the use of the bomb was justified if it spared far fewer American lives belongs more in the realms of philosophy than history. But there are tantalizing hints that Truman had some unacknowledged doubts about the morality of his decision.

Since the United States did not drop the bomb to save hundreds of thousands of American lives, as policymakers later claimed, the key question and the source of most historiographical debate is why the bomb was used. Nearly all students of the events leading to Hiroshima agree that, in addition to viewing it as the means to end the war quickly, the political implications of the bomb figured in the administration's deliberations. The consensus of the mid-1970s, which held that the bomb was used primarily for military reasons and secondarily for diplomatic ones, continues to prevail. It has been challenged and reassessed in some of its specific points, but the central theme in the consensus that has existed for the past two decades – that US officials always assumed that the bomb would be used and saw no reason not to use once it became available – remains intact. There were no moral, military, diplomatic, or bureaucratic considerations that carried enough weight to deter dropping the bomb and gaining its projected military and diplomatic benefits.

J. Samuel Walker, *Hiroshima in History and Memory,* ed. Michael J. Hogan

---

hoary: old

Activities

Writing to analyse

1   Before you start to read extracts from the above list, complete the following exercises.

    a   Choose an investigation that you have recently done in Science.

    b   Note down what you analysed and what you were seeking to find out.

    c   Identify the language, structure and organisation you need to write up a science investigation.

    d   Write up the investigation, using the language, structure and organisation you have identified.

2   **a**   As you read the extracts from the above list, make notes under two headings:

       • what the writer thinks
       • what other people quoted in the passage think.

    b   With a partner or in a small group, select one extract you have read. Draw up a final list of all your findings under these two headings.

    c   On your own, write a short analysis of the ways in which the writer uses other people's views to back up or to provide alternative views to his own.

3   **a**   After reading and studying some or all of the extracts listed on page 223, interview ten to fifteen people you know about their views on road development in your area. Try to find a cross-section of people of different ages and occupations. Make notes of what each person says.

    b   Write up your findings as an analysis of local views on road development. Make sure that all the views you found are presented in a clear and balanced way.

Writing to review

Extract 4.1:	Tending Roses	(page 184)
Extract 4.2:	Saving the World	(page 185)
Extract 4.3:	Red Hot England Fires Famous Five	(page 186)

1   Before you start to read extracts from the above list, complete the following exercises.

    a   Choose a school textbook that you are using in one of your courses this year.

    b   Make notes on the textbook under these headings:

- language level
- layout
- organisation of information
- clarity
- suitability for readership.

c Write a review of your chosen textbook for the school magazine, choosing your language and tone appropriately for a readership of fellow students and teachers.

2 a As you read the extracts from the list on page 224, make notes on them under two headings:

   • information given about the topic reviewed
   • the writer's opinion of the topic.

   b With a partner or in a small group, select one extract you have read. Compare and discuss your findings. Draw up a final list of all your notes under these two headings. Then add a short quotation from the text to illustrate each point you have made.

3 a After reading and studying some or all of the extracts listed on page 224, choose a fiction book that you have recently read and enjoyed.

   b Write a review of your chosen book to share with students in your own class. In your review you must:

   • include details of the storyline of the book
   • give your assessment of the book
   • include quotations from and references to passages in the book to back up your views
   • write in a language suitable for your intended audience.

Writing to comment

1   Before you start to read extracts from the above list, complete the following exercises.

  a   Find an editorial from each of the following:
    • a tabloid newspaper
    • a broadsheet newspaper
    • the *New Scientist* magazine.

  b   Make notes on the language and sentence structure in each of these editorials.

  c   Write three short paragraphs on the links between the language and sentence structure used in each editorial and the intended readership of the publication in which the editorial appeared.

2   a   As you read the extracts from the list, make notes on:
    • what the writers are saying
    • the facts they are commenting on
    • their points of view
    • how you can tell their points of view.

  b   With a partner or in a small group, select one extract you have read. Compare and discuss your findings, making notes where people have come to different conclusions – particularly on what the writer's point of view is.

c   On your own, write up your findings in five paragraphs. The first four should deal with the headings you have made notes on; the fifth should give your reasons for reaching the interpretation of the extract that you have given.

3 a   After reading and studying some or all of the extracts listed on page 226, research the topic of extreme sports, using books, magazines, encyclopaedias and the Internet. Make notes of the information you find.

   b   Write an article for the weekend magazine section of a broadsheet newspaper, commenting on the growing popularity of extreme sports. In your article you must:

   • use the language and sentence structure appropriate for your intended readership
   • provide clear information on extreme sports, what they are and why they are increasingly popular
   • give your own views on the reasons for their increasing popularity and whether you think it is a good or a bad thing.

Section 5

Questions comparing genres on the same theme

Travel

These extracts are concerned with travel and the traveller's experience of different places, but they are written with different purposes in mind:

- Extract 1.12 to **entertain** the reader
- Extract 2.10 to **describe** the writer's trip to Liverpool
- Extract 3.6 to **advise** travellers on the way to behave in Muslim countries
- Extract 4.11 to **analyse** what it was about Tokyo that made the author see it as the city of the future.

1 a As you read all four extracts, make notes on the language, sentence structure and tone of each extract.

b When you have read and studied all four extracts, compare and discuss your notes with a partner or in a small group. Draw up a list of the characteristics of each kind of writing under four headings:

- Writing to entertain
- Writing to describe
- Writing to advise
- Writing to analyse.

Your list of characteristics must include mention of vocabulary, sentence structure, the author's relationship with the reader (friendly, chatty, impersonal . . .), the tense of verbs, the use or absence of metaphors, similes and so on.

c   On your own, using your discussion and your list of characteristics as a guide, write about your school, the buildings and the place in which it is set in **one** of the four different ways you have been studying:

- to entertain the reader
- to describe your school and its location clearly and accurately
- to advise somebody coming to your school for the first time, telling them how to find the school and how to get around it
- to analyse the school, how it works and how it serves the community around it.

Social issues

These extracts are concerned with social issues and the writers' feelings about different aspects of social questions, but they are written with different purposes in mind:

- Extract 1.7 to **explore** the writer's experience of living on the breadline,
- Extract 2.12 to **inform** the reader about changes in air-quality in Great Britain

- Extract 3.8 to **argue** a point of view on what the writers saw as the destructive nature of global capitalism and how to respond to it
- Extract 4.5 to **analyse** the social conditions which gave rise to the homelessness crisis of the 1990s and the founding of *The Big Issue* magazine.

1 **a** As you read all four extracts, make notes on the language, sentence structure and tone of each extract.

b When you have read and studied all four extracts, compare and discuss your notes with a partner or in a small group. Draw up a list of characteristics for each kind of writing under four headings:

- Writing to explore
- Writing to inform
- Writing to argue
- Writing to analyse.

Your list of characteristics must include mention of vocabulary, sentence structure, the author's relationship with the reader (friendly, chatty, impersonal ...), the tense of verbs, the use or absence of metaphors, similes and so on.

c On your own, using your discussion and your list of characteristics as a guide, write about road safety near your school in **one** of the four different ways you have been studying:

- to explore your own experiences of traffic hazards on your way to and from school
- to inform your readers about road safety issues near your school
- to argue a case for road safety measures near your school
- to analyse the road safety issues in the area in which your school is set.

Nature

These extracts are concerned with nature and the natural world, but they are written with different purposes in mind:

* Extract 1.2 to **explore** the writer's experience of the natural world, as well as to **entertain** the reader
* Extract 2.2 to **inform** cat owners about how to look after their pets during an illness or after an accident
* Extract 3.4 to **advise** young people on what to wear and how to behave when going fox hunting
* Extract 4.7 to **comment** on the ownership of big cats as pets in America.

1 a As you read all four extracts, make notes on the language, sentence structure and tone of each extract.

   b When you have read and studied all four extracts, compare and discuss your notes with a partner or in a small group. Draw up a list of the characteristics of each kind of writing under four headings:

   * Writing to explore and entertain
   * Writing to inform
   * Writing to advise
   * Writing to comment.

Your list of characteristics must include mention of vocabulary, sentence structure, the author's relationship with the reader (friendly, chatty, impersonal . . .), the tense of verbs, the use or absence of metaphors, similes and so on.

c   On your own, using your discussion and your list of characteristics as a guide, write about pet dogs in **one** of the four different ways you have been studying:

- to explore the joys and difficulties of dog ownership in a way that will entertain your reader
- to inform your readers about the best way to care for a pet dog
- to advise somebody thinking of owning a dog about the best breed to select and how to look after it
- to comment on keeping dogs as pets.

Extreme experience

These extracts are concerned with extreme experiences of different kinds, from snowboarding to being shot, but they are written with different purposes in mind:

- Extract 1.8 to **explore** the writer's feelings about taking her mother, an Alzheimer sufferer, on a shopping trip

- Extract 2.9 to **describe** the experience of being shot
- Extract 3.3 to **persuade** tourists to travel to Canada for their winter holidays
- Extract 4.8 to **analyse** the writer's experience after severely damaging his leg in a climbing accident.

1 a As you read all four extracts, make notes on the language, sentence structure and tone of each extract.

b When you have read and studied all four extracts, compare and discuss your notes with a partner or in a small group. Draw up a list of the characteristics of each kind of writing under four headings:

- Writing to explore
- Writing to describe
- Writing to persuade
- Writing to analyse.

Your list of characteristics must include mention of vocabulary, sentence structure, the author's relationship with the reader (friendly, chatty, impersonal . . .), the tense of verbs, the use or absence of metaphors, similes and so on.

c On your own, using your discussion and your list of characteristics as a guide, write about a moment of fear in **one** of the four different ways you have been studying:

- to explore your feelings at a time when you felt acutely afraid
- to describe a place or an event that made you feel afraid
- to persuade your readers of the pleasures of feeling fear when watching a thriller or a horror movie
- to analyse what it is that makes us feel afraid.

School

These extracts are concerned with the experience of school, but they are written with different purposes in mind:

- Extract 1.3 to **explore** the writer's feelings about his education as a child in a way that will **entertain** the reader
- Extract 2.5 to **explain** the reasons behind a strike of schoolchildren
- Extract 3.1 to **advise** children on ways to get through the school day
- Extract 4.9 to **analyse** different students' responses to being at school.

1 a As you read all four extracts, make notes on the language, sentence structure and tone of each extract.

  b When you have read and studied all four extracts, compare and discuss your notes with a partner or in a small group. Draw up a list of the characteristics of each kind of writing under four headings:

- Writing to explore and entertain
- Writing to explain
- Writing to advise
- Writing to analyse.

Your list of characteristics must include mention of vocabulary, sentence structure, the author's relationship with the reader (friendly, chatty, impersonal …), the tense of verbs, the use or absence of metaphors, similes and so on.

c   On your own, using your discussion and your list of characteristics as a guide, write about the experience of school in **one** of the four different ways you have been studying:

- to explore your feelings as a school student in a way that will entertain your readers
- to explain how school works in Great Britain for a readership of students living in other countries
- to advise a new student who has come to your school on what to do and how to behave
- to analyse the experience of school for a young adult.

Childhood

These extracts are concerned with the experience of childhood, but they are written with different purposes in mind:

- Extract 1.4 to **entertain** the reader
- Extract 2.3 to **explain** what it is like to be a child living in a squatter camp in Tanzania

- Extract 3.7 to **advise** young adults and parents on the best ways to relate to each other
- Extract 4.10 to **comment** on childhood experiences a hundred years before the author was writing.

1 a As you read all four extracts, make notes on the language, sentence structure and tone of each extract.

   b When you have read and studied all four extracts, compare and discuss your notes with a partner or in a small group. Draw up a list of the characteristics of each kind of writing under four headings:

- Writing to entertain
- Writing to explain
- Writing to advise
- Writing to comment.

Your list of characteristics must include mention of vocabulary, sentence structure, the author's relationship with the reader (friendly, chatty, impersonal …), the tense of verbs, the use or absence of metaphors, similes and so on.

   c On your own, using your discussion and your list of characteristics as a guide, write about the experience of childhood in **one** of the four different ways you have been studying:

- to entertain your reader about your experiences as a child at primary school
- to explain how young children live in this country
- to advise a young adult on ways to behave at home and at school
- to comment on the treatment of children in this country.

Romance

These extracts are concerned with romance, but they are written with different purposes in mind:

- Extract 1.5 to **explore** the writer's feelings about the man she was in love with
- Extract 2.8 to **explain** to young women how to make themselves attractive to men
- Extract 3.9 to **persuade** young women that the most romantic thing they could do was to stay at home and have children
- Extract 4.6 to **analyse** the attitudes to romantic relationships on holiday as presented in teenage magazines.

1 a As you read all four extracts, make notes on the language, sentence structure and tone of each extract.

b When you have read and studied all four extracts, compare and discuss your notes with a partner or in a small group. Draw up a list of the characteristics of each kind of writing under four headings:

- Writing to explore
- Writing to explain
- Writing to persuade
- Writing to analyse.

Your list of characteristics must include mention of vocabulary, sentence structure, the author's relationship with the reader (friendly, chatty, impersonal . . .), the tense of verbs, the use or absence of metaphors, similes and so on.

c   On your own, using your discussion and your list of characteristics as a guide, write about romance in **one** of the four different ways you have been studying:

- to explore your feelings the first time you fell in love
- to explain about how romantic relationships between young adults in this country are carried out for an adult reader in the Pacific island of Tonga
- to persuade your parents or guardians to let you have a relationship with the person you love
- to analyse the nature of romantic love.

Birth and death

These extracts are concerned with birth or death or both, but they are written with different purposes in mind:

- Extract 1.10 to **explore** the writer's feelings about the death of her first baby
- Extract 2.6 to **inform** young mothers about the needs and behaviours of young babies

- Extract 3.5 to **advise** people about ways of coping with their grief on the death of a loved one
- Extract 4.4 to **comment** on a young boy's first experience of the death of an animal while out hunting.

1   **a**   As you read all four extracts, make notes on the language, sentence structure and tone of each extract.

    b   When you have read and studied all four extracts, compare and discuss your notes with a partner or in a small group. Draw up a list of the characteristics of each kind of writing under four headings:

- Writing to explore
- Writing to inform
- Writing to advise
- Writing to comment.

    Your list of characteristics must include mention of vocabulary, sentence structure, the author's relationship with the reader (friendly, chatty, impersonal . . .), the tense of verbs, the use or absence of metaphors, similes and so on.

    c   On your own, using your discussion and your list of characteristics as a guide, write about birth or death in **one** of the four different ways you have been studying:

- to explore your feelings the first time you experienced the death of a person or animal you loved
- to inform an extraterrestrial about the way human babies are born and cared for in first few years after birth

- to advise the parents of a new baby on the best way to care for their child
- to comment on the different ways there are of dealing with the death of loved ones in this country.

Hobbies and pastimes

These extracts are concerned with hobbies and pastimes, but they are written with different purposes in mind:

- Extract 1.1 to **entertain** the reader
- Extract 2.7 to **describe** a particular self-defence technique
- Extract 3.11 to **advise** readers on ways to appear to be artistically gifted
- Extract 4.1 to **review** a CD-Rom of games based around a children's book.

1 a As you read all four extracts, make notes on the language, sentence structure and tone of each extract.

b When you have read and studied all four extracts, compare and discuss your notes with a partner or in a small group. Draw up a list of the characteristics of each kind of writing under four headings:

- Writing to entertain
- Writing to describe

- Writing to advise
- Writing to review.

Your list of characteristics must include mention of vocabulary, sentence structure, the author's relationship with the reader (friendly, chatty, impersonal . . .), the tense of verbs, the use or absence of metaphors, similes and so on.

c On your own, using your discussion and your list of characteristics as a guide, write about a hobby or pastime in **one** of the four different ways you have been studying:

- to entertain your readers about the way in which a particular hobby or pastime is carried out
- to describe a particular hobby or pastime
- to advise somebody about to take up a particular hobby or pastime
- to review a magazine dedicated to a particular hobby or pastime.

Occupations

Extract 1.6:	Overgrown Boys	(page 20)
Extract 2.1:	David Beckham	(page 72)
Extract 3.2:	Which Way Now?	(page 134)
Extract 4.3	Red Hot England Fire Famous Five	(page 186)

These extracts are concerned with occupations, but they are written with different purposes in mind:

- Extract 1.6 to **explore** the feelings of adults playing amateur football in a way that will **entertain** the reader

- Extract 2.1 to **describe** David Beckham's career as a footballer
- Extract 3.2 to **advise** young people making option choices at school
- Extract 4.3 to **review** a football game.

1 **a** As you read all four extracts, make notes on the language, sentence structure and tone of each extract.

   b When you have read and studied all four extracts, compare and discuss your notes with a partner or in a small group. Draw up a list of the characteristics of each kind of writing under four headings:

   - Writing to explore/entertain
   - Writing to describe
   - Writing to advise
   - Writing to review.

   Your list of characteristics must include mention of vocabulary, sentence structure, the author's relationship with the reader (friendly, chatty, impersonal . . .), the tense of verbs, the use or absence of metaphors, similes and so on.

   c On your own, using your discussion and your list of characteristics as a guide, write about an occupation in **one** of the four different ways you have been studying:

   - to explore your feelings the first time you did a job (whether paid or not, work experience or a newspaper round or whatever)
   - to describe a particular job and the way it is carried out

- to advise somebody about to take up a job
- to review a career guidance book or leaflet about a particular job.

Science

Extract 1.9:	The Animal-Watcher	(page 36)
Extract 2.4:	Where in the World Are We?	(page 84)
Extract 3.12:	Like Human, Like Machine	(page 172)
Extract 4.2:	Saving the World	(page 185)

These extracts are concerned with topics in science, but they are written with different purposes in mind:

- Extract 1.9 to **explore** the writer's feelings about the natural world
- Extract 2.4: to **inform** the reader about the formation of our solar system
- Extract 3.12 to **argue** a case about artificial intelligence
- Extract 4.2 to **review** a science CD-Rom.

1 a As you read all four extracts, make notes on the language, sentence structure and tone of each extract.

b When you have read and studied all four extracts, compare and discuss your notes with a partner or in a small group. Draw up a list of the characteristics of each kind of writing under four headings:

- Writing to explore
- Writing to inform
- Writing to argue
- Writing to review.

Your list of characteristics must include mention of vocabulary, sentence structure, the author's relationship with the reader (friendly, chatty, impersonal . . .), the tense of verbs, the use or absence of metaphors, similes and so on.

c   On your own, using your discussion and your list of characteristics as a guide, write about a science topic in **one** of the four different ways you have been studying:

- to explore your feelings about studying a particular aspect of science
- to inform a reader about a particular science investigation and the way it is carried out
- to argue the case for or against human cloning
- to review a science extract/book.

War

These extracts are concerned with different aspects of nuclear warfare, but they are written with different purposes in mind:

- Extract 1.11 to **explore** the writer's feelings after the atom bomb was dropped on Hiroshima
- Extract 2.11 to **describe** the city after the bomb was dropped
- Extract 3.10 to **argue** the case against nuclear warfare
- Extract 4.12 to **analyse** current understanding about why the bomb was dropped.

1 **a** As you read all four extracts, make notes on the language, sentence structure and tone of each extract.

b When you have read and studied all four extracts, compare and discuss your notes with a partner or in a small group. Draw up a list of the characteristics of each kind of writing under four headings:

- Writing to explore
- Writing to describe
- Writing to argue
- Writing to analyse.

Your list of characteristics must include mention of vocabulary, sentence structure, the author's relationship with the reader (friendly, chatty, impersonal . . .), the tense of verbs, the use or absence of metaphors, similes and so on.

c On your own, using your discussion and your list of characteristics as a guide, write about war in **one** of the four different ways you have been studying:

- to explore your feelings about the rights and wrongs of going to war
- to describe to a reader the experience of soldiers on the Western Front in the First World War
- to argue a case for or against warfare
- to analyse the reasons the First World War broke out.

Acknowledgements

The publishers gratefully acknowledge the following for permission to reproduce copyright material. Every effort has been made to trace copyright holders, but in some cases it has proved impossible. The publishers would be happy to hear from any copyright holder that has not been acknowledged.

Peters Fraser & Dunlop on behalf of Clive James for 'Lollies' by Clive James, from *The New Oxford Book of English Prose*, published by Oxford University Press. Copyright © Clive James; Curtis Brown Limited, London, on behalf of The Estate of Gerald Durrell, for an extract from *My Family and Other Animals* by Gerald Durrell. Copyright © Gerald Durrell 1956; The Random House Group Limited for an extract from *Cider With Rosie* by Laurie Lee, published by Chatto & Windus; David Higham Associates Limited for an extract from *A Child's Christmas in Wales* by Dylan Thomas, published by J. M. Dent; The Random House Group Limited for an extract from *Love Lessons: A Wartime Diary* by Joan Wyndham, published by William Heinemann; *Four Four Two* for 'Overgrown boys. Armanis for goalposts. Isn't it?' by Steven Wells, from *Four Four Two*; A. M. Heath & Co. Ltd, on behalf of Bill Hamilton as the Literary Executor of the Estate of the Late Sonia Brownell Orwell and Secker & Warburg Limited, for an extract from *Down And Out In Paris and London* by George Orwell. Copyright © George Orwell 1933; Granta Books for an extract from 'Remind Me Who I Am, Again' by Linda Grant, from *Granta: The First Twenty-One Years*, published by Granta Books; Desmond Morris for an extract from *Animal Watcher* by Desmond Morris. Copyright © Desmond Morris; Sue Sabbagh for 'One in a Hundred' by Sue Sabbagh, from *World Medicine April 10th 1974*. Copyright © Sue Sabbagh; Princeton University Press for an extract from *Hiroshima: Three Witnesses* by R. Mirean, published by Princeton University Press. Copyright © 1990 by Princeton Unversity Press; A. P. Watt Limited on behalf of Jan Morris for an extract from *Destinations: Essays from Rolling Stone* by Jan Morris, published by Oxford University Press, 1982; Hodder & Stoughton Educational for an extract from *David Beckbam* by Andy Croft, published by Hodder & Stoughton, 2000; Bookmart for an extract from *The Essential Guide to Cat Care* by Amanda Edwards, published by Bookmart, 1998; IPC Syndications for 'I'm too poor to go to school' by Rafra Hason, from *MIZZ* September 5th – 18th 2001; extract from *Science Explained* by C. A. Ronan, published by Marshall Editions, 1993; BBC History Magazine for an extract from 'When the kids were united' by Deborah Partridge, from *BBC History Magazine* September 2001; Prima Baby Magazine for 'The truth about new babies' by Susan Wright, adapted from Prima Baby October 2001. Courtesy of Prima Baby Magazine © National Magazine Company; Crowood Press for an extract from *Orienteering* by Carol McNeill, published by Crowood Press; extract from *To Catch A Man* by Rehne Cloete, published by Arthur Barker, 1958; Thames & Hudson for an extract from *My Life* by Oskar Kokoschaka, translated by David Britt, published by Thames & Hudson, 1974; Black Swan for an extract from *Notes From a Small Island* by Bill Bryson. Copyright © Bill Bryson. Published by Black Swan, a division of Transworld Publishers. All rights reserved; The Random House Group Limited for an extract from *Warrior Without Weapons* by Marcel Junod, translated by Edward Fitzgerald, published by Jonathan Cape; Lisa Sykes for 'Every breath you take' by Lisa Sykes, from *Focus Magazine* September 2001. Copyright © Lisa Sykes; Comic Relief for an extract from *What a Comic Relief! The Incredibly Naughty Survive at School Handbook* by Huw Tristan Davies, Alan Rowe, Patrick Gallagher, Mark Rodgers, Ed McHenry, Michael Peek, Tony Husband and Kev F. Sutherland, published by Puffin, 1989; DfES for extracts from Which Way Now, found at www.dfes.gov.uk/whichwaynow © Crown Copyright; Phoenix Publishing for an extract from *Ski Canada* published by Phoenix Publishing on behalf of Canadian Tourism Commission. A copy can be obtained from tel:0906 871 5000; The Pony Club for an extract from *Going Fox Hunting* by Alastair Jackson, published by The British Horse Society and Pony Club, 1988; extract from *Coping With Death, a booklet for the bereaved and those who try to help them* by Leslie Scrase; Lt-Col P. G. Boxhall for 'Respecting Islam' by P. G. Boxhall, from *The Traveller's Handbook Wexas 2000*; Faber and Faber Limited for an extract from *Surviving Adolescence: A handbook for adolescents and their parents* by Peter Bruggen and Charles O'Brian, published by Faber and Faber Limited; New Internationalist for 'Resistance is the Secret of Joy' by John Jordan and Jennifer Whitney from *New Internationalist* September 2001; *Romance: An Address to Girls* by E. H. Blakeney, 1914; Taylor & Francis for an extract from *Common Sense and Nuclear Warfare* by Bertrand Russell, published by Routledge; Methuen Publishing Limited for an extract from *How To Be An Artistic Genius* by Chris Garratt, Mick Kidd & David Stafford, published by Methuen Publishing; New Scientist for 'Like Human, Like Machine' from *New Scientist* 15th September 2001; Focus Magazine for extracts adapted from *Focus Magazine* No 106 September 2001. Courtesy of Focus Magazine © National Magazine Company; The Observer for 'Germany 1 England 5' by Paul Wilson, from *The Observer* 2nd September 2001. Copyright © The Observer, 2nd September, 2001; 'Rabbiting' by J. R. Ackerley; Tessa Swithinbank for an extract from *Coming up from the streets: The Story of the Big Issue* by Tessa Swithinbank; Stephen Croft for an extract from *Romance and Sex on Holidays Abroad: A study of magazine representations* by Stephen Croft; Sonia Shah for 'Where have all the tigers gone' by Sonia Shah, from *The Ecologist* September 2001. Copyright © Sonia Shah; The Wylie Agency (UK) Limited for an extract from *A Leg To Stand On* by Dr Oliver Sacks. Copyright © Oliver Sacks 1991; extract from *Learning to Labour* by Paul E Willis, published by Saxon House 1979; William Gibson and Martha Millard Literary Agency for 'My Own Private Tokyo' by William Gibson, from *Wired* September 2001. Copyright © 2001 by William Gibson; Cambridge University Press for an extract from 'The decision to use the bomb' by Samuel Walker, from *M J Hogan Hiroshima in History and Memory 1996*. Published by Cambridge University Press.

ALSO IN

Heinemann
New Windmills

Founding Editors: Anne and Ian Serraillier

Chinua Achebe Things Fall Apart
David Almond Skellig
Maya Angelou I Know Why the Caged Bird Sings
Margaret Atwood The Handmaid's Tale
Jane Austen Pride and Prejudice
Stan Barstow Joby; A Kind of Loving
Nina Bawden Carrie's War; Kept in the Dark; The Finding; Humbug
Malorie Blackman Tell Me No Lies; Words Last Forever
Ray Bradbury The Golden Apples of the Sun
Melvin Burgess and Lee Hall Billy Elliot
Betsy Byars The Midnight Fox; The Pinballs; The Eighteenth Emergency
Victor Canning The Runaways
Susan Cooper King of Shadows
Robert Cormier We All Fall Down; Heroes
Roald Dahl Danny, The Champion of the World; The Wonderful
Story of Henry Sugar; George's Marvellous Medicine; The Witches;
Boy; Going Solo; Matilda; My Year
Anita Desai The Village by the Sea
Charles Dickens A Christmas Carol; Great Expectations; A Charles
Dickens Selection
Berlie Doherty Granny was a Buffer Girl; Street Child
Roddy Doyle Paddy Clarke Ha Ha Ha
Anne Fine The Granny Project
Jamila Gavin The Wheel of Surya
Graham Greene Brighton Rock
Ann Halam Dr Franklin's Island
Thomas Hardy The Withered Arm and Other Wessex Tales
L P Hartley The Go-Between
Ernest Hemmingway The Old Man and the Sea; A Farewell to Arms
Barry Hines A Kestrel For A Knave
Nigel Hinton Getting Free; Buddy; Buddy's Song; Out of the Darkness
Anne Holm I Am David
Janni Howker Badger on the Barge; The Nature of the Beast;
Martin Farrell

Geraldine Kaye Comfort Herself
Daniel Keyes Flowers for Algernon
Dick King-Smith The Sheep-Pig
Elizabeth Laird Red Sky in the Morning; Kiss the Dust
D H Lawrence The Fox and The Virgin and the Gypsy; Selected Tales
Harper Lee To Kill a Mockingbird
C Day Lewis The Otterbury Incident
Joan Lingard Across the Barricades; The File on Fraulein Berg
Penelope Lively The Ghost of Thomas Kempe
Jack London The Call of the Wild; White Fang
Bernard MacLaverty Cal; The Best of Bernard Mac Laverty
Jan Mark Heathrow Nights
James Vance Marshall Walkabout
Ian McEwan The Daydreamer; A Child in Time
Michael Morpurgo My Friend Walter; The Wreck of the Zanzibar;
The War of Jenkins' Ear; Why the Whales Came; Arthur, High King
of Britain; Kensuke's Kingdom; From Hereabout Hill
Beverley Naidoo No Turning Back; The Other Side of Truth
Bill Naughton The Goalkeeper's Revenge
New Windmill Book of Challenging Texts: Thoughtlines
New Windmill A Charles Dickens Selection
New Windmill Book of Classic Short Stories
New Windmill Book of Fiction and Non-fiction: Taking Off!
New Windmill Book of Humorous Stories: Don't Make Me Laugh
New Windmill Book of Nineteenth Century Short Stories
New Windmill Book of Non-fiction: Get Real!
New Windmill Book of Non-fiction: Real Lives, Real Times
New Windmill Book of Scottish Short Stories
New Windmill Book of Short Stories: A Winter's Cauldron
New Windmill Book of Short Stories: Fast and Curious
New Windmill Book of Short Stories: From Beginning to End
New Windmill Book of Short Stories: Into the Unknown
New Windmill Book of Short Stories: Tales with a Twist
New Windmill Book of Short Stories: Trouble in Two Centuries
New Windmill Book of Short Stories: Ways With Words
New Windmill Book of Stories from Many Cultures and Traditions:
Fifty-Fifty Tuti-Fruity Chocolate Chip
New Windmill Book of Stories from Many Genres: Myths, Murders
and Mysteries

How many have you read?